MW01003048

HONESTLY,
SHE DOESN'T LIVE HERE ANYMORE

A Memoir

Pamela Wick

Post Hill Press
New York • Nashville
posthillpress.com

Published in the United States of America
1 2 3 4 5 6 7 8 9 10

For Mom and Dad

"We write to taste life twice..."

—Anaïs Nin

1

My brothers were supposed to be doctors or lawyers, and I was supposed to marry one. I was that perfect plastic bride on top of the wedding cake, feet firmly planted in buttercream frosting. When I got married, it was almost like I heard a click—like something got locked into place. Robin was on the road toward becoming an international banker, which automatically made me Mrs. International Banker.

As I walk up the steps to the White House, all I can do is ask myself where it went so wrong.

"Darling, I know this is a tough time. You can stay with us as long as you need to." Dad's voice cracks like he really feels sorry for me. Six years after my wedding to the handsome Yale husband, witnessed by hundreds of family and friends, it's as if someone shot open the padlock, metal fragments splintering into the air. It's as though someone shot *me*. I got hit and fell over the edge of the wedding cake, tumbling down tiers of icing. I landed upside down, my lace gown and face smeared in sugar.

I failed my parents and their dream.

My father takes my hand as he ushers my mother up the steps to the White House. I glance down at my hand in his. I suddenly feel like a parasite that has lost its host. My parents were my original hosts, then I transferred to Robin, and now the only way to ensure my survival is to transfer back to my parents. Although I'm holding my father's hand, I can't seem to transfer back. I am lost.

Once inside, we walk past the Marine Guard to a small elevator to the family quarters. The elevator interior resembles a miniature wood-paneled library. My mother, father, and I stand close together with an attendant wearing white gloves. As the elevator doors close, I look up and spot a hatch in the wooden ceiling. I imagine getting to the elevator ceiling, squeezing myself through the chute, and escaping back to California where the sun is yellow-orange. But that would set off an alarm, the Secret Service would spring into action, the White House would be evacuated, and my shame would be huge.

I look back down and notice my mother motioning for me to smooth out the wrinkles in my silk blouse. My mother doesn't get wrinkled because she sits up straight in the car—her back doesn't touch the seat. She is perfect. But I sit against the car seat.

We step out of the elevator onto the second floor into the lavish reception hall. President Reagan greets us: "Here you are, my fellow Californians!" He looks dapper in his blazer and plaid slacks, smiling down at me with sparkly Irish eyes. Nancy, effortless in Chanel, grabs my hand and gives it a squeeze as she simultaneously engages a tall man in conversation. I fight an urge to cry, to ask Nancy (Mrs. R, we call her) if I can borrow pajamas and get into bed upstairs in the Lincoln Bedroom, where she would sit on the side of the bed and tell me I am going to be okay and have three children. I'm also angry with myself for ruining this visit to the White House. The *actual* White House. What if I pretended, just for myself, that Robin was in the bathroom the whole time? That we are still together and still in love, and he just has a bad stomach?

We are escorted to the living room for cocktails. The room is cheery: lemon-colored rug, needlepoint pillows, silver framed pictures, all punctuated by Nancy's favorite red in the sofa fabrics and chairs. The room smells of fresh flowers and Rigaud candles. Some of the guests have arrived, and drinks and canapés are being served. I take a white wine from a waiter carrying a silver tray and knock back a glass. I take another, then everything softens. I am momentarily relieved.

On the coffee table in a porcelain bowl are presidential match-books, words printed in gold: "The President's House." While no one looks, I grab a handful and stuff them into my purse. This pillaging of White House matchbooks is encouraged by Mrs. R, and, in fact, the previous Christmas when my siblings and I visited with my parents, we began our individual matchbook collections. Mrs. R cheered us on. My sister, over cocktails, said that she wanted to take a bath in the Lincoln bathroom (we like that room, because of all that gold damask fabric). So, Mrs. R got her a towel, and my sister went in and came out a half hour later, just as dinner was served, squeaky and historically clean.

We eventually make our way into the Family Dining Room for dinner and I am slightly buzzed. I tell myself Robin is still in the bath-room. Twelve of us are seated at a Federal-period mahogany table under crystal chandeliers. White House china and napkins with the presidential seal grace the dining table. I take a big breath as I sit down. I have a lump in my throat as I force a smile. On the table is a place card for the man to my immediate right, Donald Regan, Secretary of the Treasury. He is turned away from me and engaged in conver-sation with the woman to his right. I survey the table and organize the names in my mind like my house-cleaning chart, which I made to create order against the Kandinsky disorganization of color and shape inside of my brain.

Donald Regan	Secretary of the Treasury
George Will	Conservative political commentator
David Stockman	Head of Management and Budget
Bill and Sophia Casey	Head of CIA and his wife

Bill Casey is also President Reagan's former campaign manager. He often stayed at my parents' house in Los Angeles while on the road during the campaign and they became fast friends. On one of his visits, as he was walking upstairs to pack his bags, he stopped and turned back into the breakfast room where I was having coffee with Mom. He gave us a little tip: Instead of folding his clothes before placing them into his suitcase, he rolled them, which reduced wrinkling and maximized space. I was so amused by his New York accent, which sounded like rubber bands, the vowels boomeranging against consonants when he spoke. He and his wife Sophia are warm, effusive people. Looking across the table at him now, munching his watercress salad, I wonder if Casey now advises his CIA operatives about folding their clothes. The Chardonnay lifts my spirits.

My mother sits to one side of President Reagan, listening attentively to his concerns about the Soviet Union's disinformation campaign against the West. Dad joins in and tells the story of how he had recently been featured in the Russian news agency *TASS*. His aggressive policies as head of the US Information Agency make him a target of the Russians. The Russian news agency reported that "Charles Wick owns brothels in Los Angeles." My father's on-the-record response was, "Brothels? I don't even like hot soup!" Everyone bursts into laughter when he tells this story. Bill Casey has rubber bands springing out of his mouth, he's laughing so hard. No one laughs harder and longer than my father. He throws his volcanic head back, his mouth wide open; he looks like he is crying.

I scrutinize the walls wrapped with wallpaper depicting battle scenes of the American Revolution. If Robin were here, he might have appreciated the wallpaper. He is obsessed with military history and I know he would have explained the battle scene to me. But now I am suddenly fighting a battle scene in my own head. I can't stop thinking about the letter that I found in our living room, which is the reason I finally left Robin. He had written to his friend in Chicago who had just visited: "Dear Mike, I miss you. Didn't have as much fun today as when you were here." "Today," Robin spent the day with me at the zoo. So, he didn't have as much fun with me. I had no idea I was in a contest with Mike.

Had our marriage been going well, maybe I would have tried to understand the letter. But it was not going well. Robin went for drinks with his friends after work, he watched basketball games at his friends' houses when we lived in Chicago, he watched TV while we ate dinner—he did everything but talk to me. When I asked him what was on his mind he simply said, "nothing," as he pretended to play the drums on our table with one eye still on the TV. I didn't know a thing about sports, and perhaps if I would read the *New York Times* cover to cover, better understood Watergate, civil rights, women's rights, I might have been more interesting to him. But I was just me and no match for Mike. I would understand later that there were complexities that eroded our marriage, to which I contributed. I was unwilling to try things Robin enjoyed, like watching football. I also forced my idea of a proper marriage onto him by insisting we dine nightly at 6:30 p.m., that we keep our apartment tidy in case anyone dropped by, and that we spend Sundays together going to museums. We were so young, but I acted old by being rigid, where everything had to fit my idea of "perfect," and where only I was in control. Maybe that's what annoyed Robin. He wanted me to be his partner, not his mother. Now, all I can think about is the letter. An icy slush seeps into my stomach and freezes my insides. I look over at the wallpaper again and wish I were not in battle. Robin doesn't know I found the letter.

Later, during dinner, my head throbs and I fight to keep the conversation going, especially with Donald Regan next to me droning on about taxes. He manages to insert every acronym into our conversation...the FCC, the SEC, the DOJ... For me, it's as though everyone is speaking in code. Finally, he finishes offering his treatise on the Reagan tax cuts, which are part of his policies popularly called Reaganomics.

"Very interesting—thank you for that valuable information, Secretary Regan," I lie.

"KIM," he quips.

"KIM?" I ask. My sister's name is Kim. Does he know her?

"An old Wall Street expression, 'Keep It in Mind.'"

"Oh," I answer. "Good one."

He stares at me with not an ounce of humor.

I look down at my plate. A pea rolls across the china.

I turn around to him and promptly say "GTK!"

"Excuse me?" he asks.

"Good to Know!" I say, a giant grin on my face.

Donald Regan looks unamused and turns to butter his dinner roll.

It doesn't matter. This is still the highlight of my night. Am I drunk? I actually remember what it is like to be happy. I take a comedic swan dive, and, like my father, I am my own best audience.

Later, as we are leaving, I hug Mrs. R goodbye. She looks at me with warmth and empathy, her infectious laugh on pause. I know she knows I'm separated from Robin. She holds my gaze.

"My mother told you?"

She nods, taking my hands in hers. I feel like I am going to burst into tears. Nancy has that tuberose perfume smell. Her eyes are soft.

"I'm sorry," she says.

I am suddenly homesick for California. For the Reagan days there— when Mrs. R and Mom ran the chili booth at our grammar school, and when we were riding in the carpool and couldn't wait to go home to finish our homework so we could go out and play. The tuberose of Mrs. R's perfume is the jasmine outside our house in Los Angeles that covered our garden. Back then there were no acronyms, no battle-scene wallpaper, no missing husbands. Just the yellow-and-white checked wallpaper in our kitchen, the sound of crickets in summer, and the hoot of an owl at night in winter. Driving home, the night sky is dark, nearly black. I look back through the car window as the White House, lit up like a toy lantern, recedes into the distance.

2

Against a backdrop of the Jefferson Memorial, the Washington Monument, and the National Gallery, Robin and I started dating the summer of 1976. We went to concerts at the Kennedy Center. I fell in love with him during Strauss waltzes. I met his family—his father, the congressman with an office in the House Rayburn Building, where we would hang out on summer nights, watching the bicentennial fireworks illuminate the night. We'd stand on the Rayburn balcony, gazing at the humid sky. He kissed my ear with such fervor once, I lost my earring back on the congressional blue-and-gold carpet that had an emblem in the shape of an eagle. We nearly had sex on the floor of his father's office on a hot July night. The phrase "I have the floor" always held significance after that. Once when we went to get ice cream in Georgetown, Robin leaned into me and spilled chocolate on my linen shirt. He insisted on taking it to the dry cleaners—I thought that was so chivalrous.

A year later, we got married in Los Angeles. Mrs. R gave me a bridal shower and even served chili in china bowls. Ronald Reagan stopped in to say hi to the ladies and congratulated me. I felt so happy, on the tarmac of my grand life. My mother took me to Saks Fifth Avenue and we bought several nighties with bows. Mom and Mrs. R drove me to their favorite discount luggage store in Culver City, where we picked out a set of navy Lark luggage to begin my new life as Mrs. International Banker.

Now those joyous times seem ages ago. We've already been married for six years, and here we are on the brink of divorce. It has been nearly a week since I left and now I'm standing at the front door to our apartment, holding a pink box filled with glazed donuts. Is a box of pastries enough to save a marriage? Probably not. Still, I have decided to try one last time, to come and to talk to Robin, hoping that if he says the right thing, or if I say the right thing, or if somehow we connect, maybe there is still hope for the two of us.

As I stand looking at the polished wood of our front door, I realize that I have never knocked on it before. For the first time, I am a visitor to my own home. The thought makes me instantly homesick, and I feel a melancholy, heart-wrenching ache. My life is behind that door and yet here I am, holding donuts, as if I were a stranger. Our sofa and clothes and books and coffeemaker and wedding gifts, the physicality of *us*, and of course, of Robin, is separate from me as I stand outside.

After a moment, Robin comes to the door wearing sweats and a Yale T-shirt. "Glazed donuts, your favorite." I hand him the pink cardboard box, half hoping this brings us another chance. He glances at the box and looks back up at me and smiles. I fell in love with that expression, those dimples, those eyes which crinkle their own smile.

Does his smile imply we're okay? But even if he decides we're okay, I'm suddenly not so sure. What are we going to do about Mike? Should I confront him? Let's say he admits to the whole Mike thing; I don't know how I feel about a third wheel in our marriage. I don't think I'm that progressive.

In any case, Robin always glosses over everything with a Midwestern-corn-flour denial, much like my mother. And it doesn't look like today is going to be any different. He smiles as if to say, "It's all in your head," much like my mother. "We're good, you're back," his expression seems to say.

I momentarily smile, hoping to convince myself things are okay. And now I am the one in denial, a shiny, fresh denial that covers my doubt like an oversized picnic blanket.

It was his Illinois charm that first attracted me to Robin. He was from a small town called Peoria. When we met, he was standing outside in the sun in a striped Oxford shirt, tie, and khakis, chatting with fellow classmates. It was a spring afternoon and my family and I were at a Yale graduation garden party for my brother; he and Robin were in the same class. I spotted Robin from across a crowded quad and he smiled like the sun was rising. When he first said hello, his voice was soft and smooth like buttermilk. It was as if the farm air blew into his child-hood room at night and bathed him in goodness, and it was this aura he exuded that made me feel safe around him. Sweet grass and tilled soil, there he was as he spoke, wrapping his voice around his words with respect.

As Robin and I walk toward the kitchen in our apartment, the memories fade. Our floral sofa in the living room looks just the same as it did the previous week when I had been sobbing so hard, I thought the floral pattern would run. The overstuffed chairs remain in place, holding their collective breath as they wait for life to resume. I can't seem to remember why I left Robin and our apartment. Maybe everything had been perfect; maybe I just didn't realize.

We sit on our kitchen floor, facing each other. This is where I had cooked so many perfect meals for the both of us and perfected Julia Child's beef stew, which Robin devoured.

"You just need to come back," he says, fidgeting with his wedding ring. I so badly want to tell him that I'd love to, but there is the matter of the letter to Mike that I haven't mentioned yet.

"We don't talk. We never talk. In the morning. After work," I say, hoping he'll comfort me, promise that he'll make an effort to change.

"We talk about stuff."

"Not our feelings. What's going on in here." I motion to my chest. "The TV's always on. Basketball. Football. You're glued to the TV. I have to talk to you during the commercials." If he meets me halfway, I'm willing to watch sports with him, if that's what it takes to improve our relationship.

"You're telling me not to watch TV?"

Robin had completely missed the point. Does he not get that it's not the television that I have a problem with? I just want him to be more present so I don't have to wait for commercials to speak to him. I wonder what his idea of a marriage is.

"I'm saying we need to talk more."

He sighs, exasperated, but I don't want to give up just yet. I want him to understand that things need to change between us if we want our relationship to improve.

"You're gone so much." I blame him, without acknowledging my part, and he gets defensive.

"I have to travel for my job."

Robin's not wrong. He does have to travel for work, but it still feels to me like it's all his fault.

"But you have a meeting on a Thursday and then you stay away the weekend."

"That was in Chicago. I stay with Mike and Jody." There. He said it. Mike. Dear Mike. The letter.

"Mike. You. The letter to him. I found it. I read it."

He looks at me, blankly.

I look over at him. He stares off, gnawing on his fingernail. He is so handsome. Boyishly so. My heart beats too fast.

"You had more fun with Mike?"

"What?"

"In the letter. 'Went to the zoo today. Didn't have as much fun as when I went with you.'" I wait for a reply.

He looks off. Then turns back to me. "I still love you."

11

I want to jump into his arms and to feel safe again. I want to walk to the zoo together, feed the penguins, then come home, eat grilled cheese sandwiches, and maybe have sex. But as I stare at the unopened donut box between us, I know it's over.

"I have to go." I get up and go to the bedroom to pack some clothes. Our bed is unmade. I open the closet door and stare at my skirts and blazers. How much will I need? I'm overwhelmed. I squish several skirts into my Lark suitcase and pull down another one for my shoes and blazers. It chokes me up to think these suitcases were for my new married life and now they are for...what? My divorced single life?

I drive back into my parents' long driveway and stop the car in front of their modern concrete-and-glass house. I get out, pick up my suitcases, and walk a few steps. Then I sit down on the driveway pavement, squeezing my knees to my chest. I am having a panic attack. Sounds muffle, birds stop chirping, crunchy leaves are silent. Just the sound of my fiercely beating heart fending off a tsunami of fear. I'm perspiring and sweat is seeping through my shirt. I wipe back my sticky hair and lick salty sweat off my upper lip.

3

"Here, have some water," my mother says as she hands me a glass. We stand in front of the sink in the kitchen, my suitcases on the floor. She is dressed elegantly in slacks and a cashmere sweater and the midday light shines on her face.

"Honey, this too shall pass, it's better you know now, and it is so sad."

When is Robin going to tell his parents about us? I imagine he will wait as long as he possibly can; I know he will pretend everything is normal till then. What are they going to do about the family Christmas card? I imagine it's too late to airbrush me out. The annual photo was recently taken in his father's congressional office, his family and I standing under framed photographs of politicians, next to an American flag. The photo is the front of a glossy holiday card, with a yearly update inside encircled by holly berries. How sad to think of the edited text for next year, "...our son Robin is working hard at his banking job and enjoying intramural office sports." Maybe there'd be no mention of our divorce. I would merely no longer be in the family photo. Where I once stood, there would be a small potted tree with twinkle lights.

"We're having hamburgers for dinner, sound good?" Mom is revving back up to optimistic as she turns toward the refrigerator.

"Your father should be home later. He had a meeting with his co-deputy."

So that's it. I am crossing over to the next chapter of my life. I pick up my suitcases and wander out of the kitchen and toward the long hallway with floor-to-ceiling windows in the direction of the guest room, my new home. The rest of the afternoon I spend putting away my clothes and sleeping, dreaming of the life I am leaving as I toss and turn with the afternoon light filtering into the room. Outside, fall leaves descend from their branches on this sad October day.

Later, the smell of grilled onion and hamburgers leads me into the kitchen. Cody is near the stove; he spots me and trots over, making a beeline for my crotch, his usual way of greeting me. My parents got this Doberman for security reasons, but he himself is a security risk. The two sisters, who live in the house and work for my parents, nicknamed him "Mr. Horny." Achin, the older sister, is at the sink. She looks over at Cody and notices him goosing me.

"Mr. Horny! No!" she scolds.

I laugh, which feels so good. My mother shakes her head in feigned disgust and then my father walks into the kitchen, also led by his nose. He grabs a pickle from a jar on the counter and tells me how sorry he is, that Mom told him about my meeting with Robin. "Look, you'll get through this. It's going to take time. Honestly, I think you did the right thing. We like Robin a lot, but it isn't a good situation anymore. You just focus on you now; you'll work out all the details." I watch my father's face as he talks. On one hand he can be so tough, but on the other he is also deeply empathic.

"I think we should wait for Robin to tell them, then your mother and I will follow up with a call." He seems concerned about Robin's parents, whom we like a lot.

My parents have always been close to Robin's family. The first time his parents walked into our house, my father proceeded to play the University of Illinois fight song on his baby grand piano. (Dad, in addition to being a lawyer, is a trained musician. So it was a hit.) The mutual fondness was instantaneous. The fact that Robin's father was the Republican minority leader in the House of Representatives and my father was a member of Ronald Reagan's kitchen cabinet solidified their friendship.

Over dinner, I listen to my parents talk about Washington, their social calendar, upcoming cocktail parties, the Soviet Union, the latest piece in the style section of *The Washington Post*. I can't seem to care about these things. In California, we never spoke about social calendars or the Soviet Union. Our home in Los Angeles was a sprawling traditional my parents bought from Lana Turner in the '50s. Tour buses routinely traveled down the street and idled in front of our house. "This is the house of famed actress Lana Turner," the tour guide's voice would boom into our driveway. My father got so tired of the intrusion, he had a sign permanently planted in front of our large hedges, which stated in an elegant script, "Honestly, She Doesn't Live Here Anymore."

Our life in Southern California was filled with the "coo, coo" of mourning doves, the whooshing of traffic on Sunset Boulevard, and the sweet scent of night-blooming jasmine. If I could go back to our house in Los Angeles now, I think I'd still be homesick. I would recognize where I grew up, but I would no longer be a part of it. A piercing, unrelenting longing is my new home. I am homesick for Robin and our apartment and our stuff. I imagine him eating dinner by himself, watching TV. Is he homesick for me?

This, my first night with the knowledge my marriage is over, feels like a dream. Or, more accurately, it feels like the end of a dream.

4

People don't get divorced in my family. In fact, no one I knew got divorced when I was growing up. Well, there was one girl—Joan Rinde. I went to school with her at Westlake. Her brother Rob attended school with my brothers. One day Joan came to school, and it looked like she had been crying. Her face was red and she wiped her eyes with the sleeve of her uniform blouse. Then she told someone her parents were divorcing and soon the news was all over school. I would see her walking down the halls, not talking to anyone, her head hanging down. Her mother, Mrs. Rinde, would stand alone at the school's open house. Mrs. Rinde always wore black as if she were at a funeral, as if being divorced was a kind of memorial to her former, happy life.

One time she and the other parents were in our geography class admiring our papier-mâché Africa relief maps. I noticed Mrs. Rinde looking around, as if waiting for her husband, Joan's father, to show up. But why would he? They were divorced. To my sixteen-year-old self, divorce seemed a sort of death. Marriage is supposed to be forever.

Now, the only evidence that I was ever married is a slight tan line where my wedding ring used to be. We still need to split our wedding gifts, but everything else has been thrown out or given away. It amazes me how a life can be disassembled so quickly, tossed into boxes and be made to suddenly disappear. I catch myself rubbing the little white stripe on my finger, massaging the skin until the white turns red and looks less noticeable. I'm trying to get used to the day when the white no longer exists, when the last lingering evidence has completely faded away.

My parents are kind. My mother keeps saying, "This too shall pass," and my father goes out of his way to talk to me more, to ask how I'm doing. But I know I have disappointed them. They had expectations for me, and since I was little, I knew in no uncertain terms what those were. I was going to be like my mother, get married, have perfect children, and support my husband's career. My sisters and I trained at an early age. Every night after dinner, we cleared the table and did the dishes while our brothers remained at the table talking to our father about "important things." We all studied hard, but my brothers had to get As—they knew that they would apply to law school. My sisters and I did not consider going to graduate school. After all, we didn't need a career in our future. It was understood that we would work until we got married. After that, domestic life and children would be the center of our world.

So, I hide my true feelings from my parents. I tell them I'm okay, that I am feeling like I have done the right thing leaving my marriage. I put on a happy face. I try to laugh extra hard at my father's jokes, act interested when my mother shows me a new outfit she bought herself or tells me about an upcoming gala at Ford's Theatre. I try to paint a rosy picture. I feel like I want to make everything okay and that it is expected of me to do so. In my family, we see the glass as half full. My parents are survivors.

My sister Cindy is the only one I confide in, even though she is younger than me. Since we were little, we have told each other all our secrets. Cindy is an artist and her drawings have even been published in the *New York Times*. She isn't married yet and isn't bound by the responsibilities of "being a wife." She works at a film-advertising firm in the Paramount Building in New York City. I've always been fascinated by what she does for a living—creating movie posters and coming up with taglines for films. She's just finished the poster for *Mr. Mom* with Teri Garr and Michael Keaton, a film about a father losing his job and his wife finding a job, leaving him at home with the kids. The tagline is, "When Mom goes to work, Dad goes berserk."

I imagine her life, single in her twenties, walking down 78th Street, backpack slung over her shoulder, wool cap over her long hair. On the weekends she and her work friends go out to hip restaurants and stay out all night.

Cindy calls me every morning and she has this ability, much like our mother, to view situations through the lens of optimism. When we were kids, on Sunday nights our family watched *The F.B.I.* and *Bonanza* in our parents' bedroom. Cindy and I would sit on the floor, sketching fashion models on pads of paper. She'd glance over at my drawing and say she loved it. But I knew my drawing wasn't of the same caliber as hers. Yet she made me feel talented. She's always been like that, propping me up.

"Checking in," she says today. Her tone is warm and caring. I tell her that the divorce makes me feel like the dream has ended. She replies without hesitating: "I feel like you just woke up."

Maybe Cindy is right.

"Pam, you need a life of your own. Leave Mom and Dad. Get yourself a job," Cindy tells me. I think about it and I find myself wishing that I hadn't gotten married so early. I could have explored a career, like Cindy has. Because I was her oldest daughter, my mother wanted to mold me, and I became her project. I was so young and impressionable it was easy for her to do that, and I grew up believing that the correct way to live life was to live like her. I always knew I would get married first—my mother and I talked about it so many times that I hadn't had a chance to imagine an alternative future. My younger sisters escaped this expectation and now have lives I wish I had.

How can I suddenly leave my hosts and survive by myself? Cindy makes it sound so simple, but the thought of showing up somewhere and being effective seems beyond my grasp at the moment. I spend much of my time in bed, which has become my second skin, my head buried beneath the pillows so I can hardly breathe.

"It will get you out of the house. You can start over."

For a moment, I can visualize an image of me, briefcase in hand, blazer with shoulder pads and skirt, walking down a busy street to my office, purposeful and belonging.

But the reality of my circumstances quickly drops me back to earth. Who would hire me? What am I possibly qualified to do? I have spent my life learning how to throw a dinner party and how to line up the salad fork with the entrée fork. No one has ever told me that I could stand up in front of a boardroom.

5

My working history consists of a job as a clerk at a French clothing boutique in Beverly Hills, a salesgirl at Saks Fifth Avenue, and a floating temporary secretary at the Art Institute in Chicago. My experiences don't involve the kind of skills that are needed in jobs in Washington. My previous jobs didn't involve controversy, unless you thought it was controversial to mix a black blazer with a blue skirt. They didn't deal with "issues" and consequential decisions made here in the nation's capital. There was no State Department, no Pentagon, no White House.

Instead, there was Tina Turner, the Queen of Rock 'n' Roll. On my first day on the job at Saks, in Better Sportswear, I spotted her. I remember smiling so wide it actually hurt my face. I wanted to appear friendly. I helped her by hauling armloads of clothes into her dressing room. Turner was so fun. She laughed a lot as she tried on designer jogging suits, a metallic beaded jacket, and a hot pink tank top with feathers. When she finally decided what to buy, I got so baffled ringing her up I had to ask for help from a more experienced colleague. This was my very first transaction. It was huge. The biggest in our department all month. I had forgotten I was on commission even though I had, no doubt, been told about it. I guess it just hadn't sunk in. I was more concerned with memorizing the racks of inventory and smiling properly.

My job didn't last long. I got fired when my supervisor called our home one Saturday. She assumed I was home because I had called in sick that morning. Instead, I had gone to the beach—which is exactly what our housekeeper said when she answered the phone: "I'm sorry, she's at the beach." When my father found out he yelled at me for nearly a half hour. He was furious and told me how irresponsible I was and that I must have "cauliflower ears" because I'd been told so many times being responsible is essential. I was eighteen years old and my father grounded me for a month. I didn't go to the beach for the rest of the summer.

I learned from my mistake and was very responsible at my next job. I was a temp assistant in the Prints and Drawings department at the Art Institute of Chicago, the city where Robin and I lived. I came to work on time, left on time, and only took off on legal holidays. I sat at a desk in a stuffy room while one of my coworkers chain-smoked Camels. My eyes would water as I filed documents for an upcoming show catalogue. Every so often, the curator, Mr. Mars, would call out from his office, "Girls, I need a coffee, please." He was very thin, his voice soft, and his skin translucent. He reminded me of a marble statue in the permanent collection.

Now, I'm not sure what to do. I want so badly to get out of the house. I want to live on my own and be independent like my sister Cindy, but I can't quite see the path or gather the courage. Would it be wrong to ask my parents for help? For help escaping their grasp? The very idea makes me laugh. Yet, it's the only idea I have.

When I finally get up the courage to ask, my father couldn't be happier. He is in his element. He paces back and forth excitedly in my parents' bedroom. He grabs a Dictaphone and speaks into the small machine, enunciating clearly, not wanting to lose a single idea that is bouncing around in his head.

"Contacts for Pam job. Create a file. Call it Pam's employment; no, Pam's career prospects; no, Pam's future. Then, five sub-files. Arts, foreign policy, public relations, diplomacy, and, uh, let's see, Motion Picture Association; I'll give Jack Valenti a call."

Dad continues reeling off names and they all blur together. Bob Gray, Henry Rogers, Mark Seigel. All "the Top People." My mother and I watch from our seats on overstuffed chairs.

"Honey, what about that nice man who works at the diplomacy at State?" My mom is Midwestern calm, her blonde hair perfectly coiffed. She doesn't burst with energy like my father, but I know the inside of her head is exploding with ideas, too. I can tell she secretly smoked a cigarette because she is spraying a blast of Binaca into her wide-open mouth, quickly closing it and hiding evidence. Tobacco is supposed to add to her calm and, at the same time, give her momentum. I've seen it hundreds of times. Whether she is picking out ground beef for dinner or a pearl necklace for a gown. (She knows she's not supposed to smoke, so cigarettes have become a covert operation.)

"Mary Jane, ask Nancy Reagan about that lobbying firm—great gal runs the place," my father looks up from his Dictaphone.

My parents are talking about the lobbying firm of Wexler, Reynolds, Harrison & Schule, a high-powered lobbying group.

"Charles, I already did. It's Nancy Reynolds."

I think about how odd it is that there are two Nancys involved. How do they refer to one another? Do they laugh when they greet each other saying "Hi, Nancy," and "Hi back, Nancy?"

After deciding to set me up a meeting with Nancy Reynolds, my parents go on to the next possibility. Selwa Roosevelt, more popularly known as "Lucky" Roosevelt, is married to a grandson of President Theodore Roosevelt. She is also head of Protocol at the State Department. How apt that her name is Lucky. My father thinks I would be great in Protocol because he says I'm smart and I make a good impression on people. I wonder what it would be like to work for Lucky Roosevelt.

Soon my father is rattling off more names into his Dictaphone. There are Johns and Sams and Rogers and someone with the cumbersome name of Stassinopoulos.

It's as if my parents are layering a giant canvas with paint, creating a colorful picture of my future employment. I am a mere observer in this process—I only listen and watch. I'm like Cody the Doberman, who follows my father with his eyes, knowing something serious is happening but not completely understanding what. Cody and I both wait patiently. Anything I had to say would merely be an interruption.

Even before I got divorced, I *was* planning on getting a job. But back then it was only going to be to supplement Robin's income, somewhere to trot out my Brooks Brothers blazers until we had kids. Then my real job would start. I was already a wife; I'd be a mother sooner than later. In addition to our social calendar, I would organize the feeding schedule, food, and diapers, all the while managing tennis and charity work. Once, I had been looking forward to this. A full life.

My parents are doing more than just helping me find a job. They are figuring it out for me. They have always figured everything out, including my wedding. My father chose the music, Bach's *Jesu, Joy of Man's Desire* (ironically). My mother figured out my dress, my china, how we would raise our future children. I listen as I wait for them to plan the next chapter of my life, and while I am very grateful, I feel equally lost.

* * *

NANCY REYNOLDS HAS PIERCING BLUE EYES. She is blonde, warm and friendly, and has a dazzling smile. (I didn't get a meeting with Lucky Roosevelt; she had just hired someone.) Before we get down to the actual interview, we chat about the Reagans. I learn that Nancy was Ronald Reagan's press secretary for two terms when he was Governor of California, and that she and Mrs. R have been close ever since. Nancy tells me she and my parents even worked together when she was on

President Reagan's transition team. I start to relax because she is treating me like we're old friends.

Still, I know this is business—the constant phone ringing outside her office, the newspapers stacked on her desk, her assistants rushing in and out, clients walking into the front lobby of the office suite. I wonder how much of her time I'm taking up and worry that I'll make her late for some important appointment.

I realize that this interview is merely a formality. It's the way Nancy leans forward and says, "I think you'd do great here," as if she already decided to hire me before I walked in. I am taken aback; it is all so quick. I wonder if she realizes I know very little about lobbying? And yet she seems least worried as she tells me what I'd be doing.

"We need someone in a junior position. We're so busy."

She explains that I would be helping the partners, taking notes in meetings, preparing briefing materials, escorting VIPs to the Hill (short for Capitol Hill, at least it's not an acronym) and attending events on behalf of the firm.

"You'd fill in as needed. It can get chaotic, but it's fun," she looks at me, her blue eyes flashing. "What do you think?"

Should I tell her that I think that I am unqualified for the job? Being here is all too intimidating, but I thank her and accept the job anyway.

I got the job because of my parents. Because of the Reagans. I know this is how Washington works, and yet I feel guilty. I didn't do *anything* to get this job. I just put on a blazer and I showed up. I think of the people who are qualified for and deserving of this job. If they really needed someone to do this job, it wouldn't be me. They've created this role just to fit me in.

I walk down the street along with the other businesspeople leaving their offices for lunch. There are women in skirts and high heels, strands of pearls that scream preppy. I am in awe of them, of the way they seemingly know they belong here.

Two men step off the sidewalk to buy a newspaper. So, this is what busy important people do: They read the paper, they keep up on events, they know the names of congressmen and the bills that are on the floor.

"*The Post*," I say to the scruffy guy behind the counter. Not "the *Washington Post*," or "the *New York Post*," just "*The Post*." I feel a tinge of excitement for just a moment. I will start learning by reading the newspaper. All of it. The news guy and I exchange a knowing glance—I am a Washingtonian and to him I might even be important. Without a further look, I pick up the paper, hand the guy some coins, and walk down the street toward the business people on the sidewalk, blending seamlessly into the crowd.

* * *

I TAKE THE REST OF THE WEEK TO PREPARE FOR MY NEW JOB. I go to the library. I don't even know what exactly a lobbyist is. The term came from the British Parliament, where wheeling and dealing took place in lobbies outside the chambers. I write all this in a spiral notebook and highlight my own sentences. I had taken a political science class at Berkeley, but I retained very little of the information. Republican, Democrat, Speaker of the House, majority leader—I just wasn't interested. Now the words buzz in my head.

One day while in a cab going to meet my mother for lunch in Georgetown, I notice the cabbie has a business book next to him on the front seat: *United States Government*. He tells me he is in school at George Washington (GW) University, and this is his textbook. I write down the name in my spiral notebook. I go to GW and buy the identical book.

This book becomes my bible. At night, when my parents aren't out for dinner or attending events, which is rare, I tell them what I'm learning, and Dad tells me not to worry. "You're not expected to know everything." But I don't feel this way. I know *nothing* and my parents don't understand. How do they have so much confidence in me? I continue highlighting my business book in bed most nights, and then I cry about Robin.

I wake up one morning and decide to make flash cards and paste them to my bathroom mirror. As I brush my teeth, I quiz myself. I know that Tip O'Neill is the Speaker of the House and that Howard Baker is the majority leader. I will learn everything I can. I will make myself indispensable.

6

My first week is a flurry of new. New colleagues, new bosses, new office, and new sadness. My busyness from the previous week, from learning and reading, has vanished. I'm uncomfortable, anxious, and anticipatory. This new is laced with loss. All I think about is Robin. He *should* be hearing about my day. Robin *should* be meeting my new colleagues at a work cocktail event. Robin *should* sit down to dinner with me and explain how a bill gets passed in Congress. Robin *should* be my husband. My job feels so much about the loss of him. And I can't concentrate on what I'm actually supposed to be doing: filling out W-2 forms, organizing my new office, learning about what I'm supposed to know.

And now I'm in the end stall in the bathroom, crying. It's only Tuesday morning. I couldn't make it to my next meeting without running in here. It's as though I will implode from the pressure, exploding inward to nothing but a blazer with shoulder pads. Tears flood down my face and I lean into the pale-yellow wall, wishing I could dissolve into little molecules of yellow pigment so I wouldn't have to be a person, so I wouldn't have to feel. I would just exist—a palette of paint spread over drywall.

Once I've let it all out, I splash cold water on my face and pat on some base makeup to even out my skin tone. One last glance in the mirror, then I leave.

As I head back down the hallway, I lower my head so no one will notice me. Then out of the corner of my eye I spot one of my new colleagues, Pam Curtis, walking toward me. She is older, in her late thirties, smartly dressed. I'm prepared to step by her, but she stops.

"Rough first day?" she says knowingly, out of the blue.

Can she tell I've been crying? Does she think less of me for it?

"It'll get easier," she says with warmth in her eyes.

Not wanting to tell her about Robin, I mention work.

"I'm pretty confused about everything, to be honest."

There is something about the way she looks at me that tells me she will be someone I can confide in. Her name is Pam, too. Maybe we will be good friends. Not now, but in time, possibly.

"We can grab lunch and talk about it, if you like."

Wait, did I just make a new friend? I'm immediately tempted to tell Robin about her. But then I remember there is no Robin anymore.

7

I wish I could get out of my work commitment today. But I know it's impossible, this being my first week on the job. I'm not feeling up to attending the Republican Women's luncheon, which is apparently a big honor. I am representing our firm, and Pam told me that this lunch is for congressional wives—but that sometimes others are invited. "These women are an important way to building bridges with their husbands." So, my job is to meet and greet, and to make friends so that I can lunch with a congressional wife who will connect me with her husband, or when I meet a congressman I can say, "I chatted with your wife at the luncheon, she is lovely." A strategic plan for "getting to know you."

So why does this feel so difficult? Because my eyes are puffy from crying all night, and I feel so down. But I'm wearing my Anne Klein red wool gabardine power suit, and my mother lent me her designer bag with a clasp in the shape of a bumblebee. This spells success, I tell myself, in spite of my puffy eyes. I walk into the Congressional Club, a Beaux-Arts building on New Hampshire Avenue featuring magnificent floor-to-ceiling windows, striated wallpaper, American oil paintings, and tables with bright, floral centerpieces. This rivals the Library of Congress and the White House—it is so spectacular. I see women in nice dresses and skirts and blazers sip white wine as they mingle. I can do this.

I take a big breath as I walk up to the check-in table, forcing a smile on my face.

"Your name, please?"

I stop for a minute; what *is* my name? Don't I want to change it back to Pamela Wick now that I'm getting divorced? I've thought I would, but now I wonder about *when*. I look back at her like she'll tell me the answer, then I give her my married name, Pamela Michel.

I take my name tag, pin it to my jacket, and begin to circulate. I glance around at the sea of colorful dresses and feel overwhelmed by the scent of perfume. *Come on, you have to do your job*, I chastise myself. I grab a drink and look for my table. I walk by some wives chatting and I smile widely to appear like a fun person. "Hi, nice to meet you."

As I find my table, I notice at each place is a *Congressional Club Cook Book* wrapped in a bow. I own one of these cookbooks already. It was a gift from Robin's mother when we got married. The annual book is a club fundraising effort. The recipes are from the First Ladies of Washington, DC, spouses, friends, and family. They range from Mary (Mrs. John Stennis) from Mississippi's Mushroom Soup Meatloaf and Alice (Mrs. H. Martin Lancaster) from North Carolina's Candy Bar Cheesecake, to Phyllis (Mrs. James Olin) from Virginia's Spinach Balls, to Joan (Mrs. Wally Herger) from California's Tortilla Pinwheels. I never used the cookbook and I always felt bad about never trying one of the dishes, like I was being disloyal to my mother-in-law. I mutter that I have the cookbook, to make conversation. The woman sitting next to me perks up.

"You have the cookbook already?" She stares at my name tag.

"Yes, the 1977 version. This is more updated," I say, trying to be friendly.

"Wait. Wait," she cocks her head to the side, thinking.

"Your name, Michel. Aren't you married to...?"

She snaps her fingers. "Umm...I know...let me think a minute...."

"I'm not a wife of a congressman, just a guest," I smile as I unwrap my cookbook hoping the conversation will move away from me. It doesn't.

"But wait, Michel...are you related to Bob Michel?"

My soon-to-be-former father-in-law Bob Michel is a rock star to this crowd as the deeply respected Republican leader in the House of Representatives. I peek at the woman's name tag. Mary is the wife of a congressman from Nebraska. As she looks at me, I wonder how I could end the conversation. I wish she would close her surprised mouth because she looks like Edvard Munch's *The Scream.*

"Is Bob Michel *your* father-in-law?" Another woman leans forward across the table.

No! Why did this woman have to remember? I don't want to be known as Bob Michel's daughter-in-law. I want to be known for me, for who *I* am. But who am I really without these connections? Without my father, Robin's father, the Reagans? Nothing!

"I *knew* it!" Mary claps her hands together. "I saw you in their family Christmas card," she says, realizing. The same Christmas card where my photo will be replaced next year with a small potted tree with twinkle lights.

"My husband idolizes Bob Michel; they're a wonderful family," another wife says a little too loudly. It's true that they are a wonderful family, but I'm not a part of it anymore. In any case, I wouldn't call Robin "wonderful." Not anymore.

"I'm separated," I say evenly. The table goes silent. I don't want their pity, I just want them to stop talking about it.

"Oh, that's terrible. I am so sorry." Mary's face falls.

"I'm good." I try to remain cheerful.

"Oh, my God, that's it! Your father is Charles Wick!" bursts Mary.

The women at the table stare at me, their eyelids not blinking.

"You have Christmas with the Reagans."

There it goes! First my father, then my father-in-law, and now the Reagans. By now I am cringing. It's like they're opening one of those Russian nesting dolls. I am hiding deep inside. They keep going, the hand-painted dolls getting smaller and smaller until there is me, tiny, shrunk down to a miniature awkward self. As the facts are unearthed, there is a whipped-up fervor at the table. My cheerful self chats away. "Yes, my mom met Mrs. Reagan in our carpool in grade school. Patti was in my brother's class. Yes, Ron Jr. is an actual ballet dancer." The unhappy me is the tiny Russian doll in fetal position. I am relieved when the presentation begins. The topic is "The First Ladies Gown Collection" and the curator of the collection speaks animatedly along with a slide show.

There are gowns from Lady Bird Johnson and Eleanor Roosevelt. But what gets the most oohs and aaahs is a red gown from Jackie O. These women can never get enough of Jackie O.

8

"I'm fighting like hell to get the ERA ratified. I know President Reagan is your family friend, but he hasn't done a lot for women."

Pam's comment takes me off guard. We are sitting at a table in a crowded downtown restaurant. I've never really thought about women's issues—or politics, for that matter. Growing up, my family spent a lot of time talking about movies, our school projects, our brothers, and music. I remember our father playing a flawless "Rhapsody in Blue." Music was his passion. My mother, however, was a supporter of Barry Goldwater, the former Arizona senator and presidential candidate, and admired his service in the Air Force reserve. She even kept a can of "Gold Water" in our refrigerator in his honor. I was nine years old at the time and all I wanted was to taste the fizzy drink.

My father, on the other hand, was a Democrat; that is, until my parents became friends with the Reagans. Post governorship of California, Dad got the idea that Reagan should make a run in the primary for the presidency. I remember my parents coming home from dinner with the Reagans; they were so excited. Dad believed that Ronald Reagan could defeat then-president Jimmy Carter. He thought he had possibly convinced Reagan to consider running for office.

Sitting across from Pam, I envy her colorful scarf, her pearls, her hair—which is short and feminine. I wonder if she thinks I am a bit

33

dowdy, in my turtleneck and skirt and brown penny loafers. I wonder if she can tell I'm depressed.

I want to say something intelligent, something that lets Pam know I'm not completely ignorant when it comes to politics. Just then, she gets distracted by a group of men in business suits who've walked into the restaurant.

"Fabulous; what luck!" she says.

To my utter horror, I realize she is staring at my father-in-law, Congressman Bob Michel.

The problem is that I have yet to tell my in-laws that I am getting a divorce from their son. I wanted Robin to tell them, but he kept putting it off. Avoiding confrontation is his specialty.

Then Pam looks over at me. "What are you doing?!"

I'm hiding behind my menu.

My father-in-law and the group of men head toward our table, ushered by the maître d'.

"You have to introduce me. He's key to the upcoming vote in the House on business regs!" Pam says.

She starts to get up, her eyes glued to my approaching father-in-law.

"Pam, no!" I nearly yell from behind my menu. My mind swirls. I can't say hi to him. How do I pretend that everything is fine? And what if he asks me how Robin is doing? Do I lie and say he's fine? Or maybe I say Robin's super busy at work and I barely see him.

But my father-in-law spots me.

"Hey, look who's here!" he says loudly, his face beaming. He stops and opens his arms to greet me. The people surrounding him part like the Red Sea.

I give my father-in-law a hug. He is a big bear of a man, so joyous when he sees me. He is always the center of a crowd, often singing his baritone rendition of "Old Man River" and other songs to his colleagues in Congress.

"So great to see you! This is my colleague, Pam Curtis."

He grabs Pam's hand and shakes it warmly.

"You're taking good care of our Pam, I hope."

"Yes," Pam says. "We are so lucky to have her."

"I'm lucky to have her as my daughter-in-law." He smiles.

I don't know what to do. I feel like bursting into tears. I am devastated, looking at his cheery face, knowing that I am about to tear his family apart. His son will no longer have a wife, and he will no longer have a daughter-in-law. I hate myself for not being able to make my marriage work, for not trying to understand Robin better, for not being more accommodating.

In spite of how torturous this is for me, Pam is ecstatic about meeting my father-in-law. "Listen," she says to him, "May I call your office and come in to talk to your finance person about HR2380? We're representing Bristol." She's referring to a bill on the environment.

"Of course. Call and ask for Ed Sheehan. Tell him I recommended you."

For Pam, being able to meet with my father-in-law's key aide at his personal request, and advocate for her client, is a major coup—one that might not have happened without me. In Washington, "who you know" is invaluable currency.

My father-in-law turns back to me. "When are you kids coming over to dinner? Sunday? We'll take you out. Maybe your folks could join us? Gee, that'd be fun."

I look at him, dumbfounded. It is such a normal question but suddenly it feels like a punch to my stomach.

"Sunday? Great," I say, utterly panicked, not knowing how else to respond.

* * *

I AM DREADING THE CONVERSATION THAT IS ABOUT TO TAKE PLACE. All I can think is that I want it to be over. But it is the right thing to do, and my in-laws deserve to know. Still, as I walk up the front steps of their townhouse, it feels as if I'm about to toss a grenade through their front door.

I usually try to say things that make people happy and I have always been this way. Maybe because our father was prone to explosions of anger. I never wanted to say the wrong thing. So, instead of saying what I really thought or truly needed, I said nice things, happy things.

My mother-in-law Corinne greets me with her cheerful face.

"Hi! Honey, where's Robbie?" She looks over my shoulder, searching for her son.

"He couldn't come. It's just me." This is just the beginning of the bad news, I think.

"Well, we love seeing you!"

I walk into their kitchen; her familiar cigarette rests on a counter ashtray. I think of all the times I have sat in this kitchen, eating my mother-in-law's green bean casseroles, picking off the canned onion rings while she asked if Robin and I had enough laundry soap because she bought too much on sale. Now looking at her, I realize she has no idea that her world is about to change. Her youngest son will be getting divorced.

My father-in-law steps in from the living room.

"Well, look who's here!" The sound of his booming voice saddens me. He gives me an enthusiastic hug. "Where's Rob?"

"He couldn't come." I hesitate. "I need to talk to you guys."

There is a moment of silence, and the confusion on their faces tears me apart. I want to lie, to tell them that I'd come to announce I was pregnant with their first grandchild. I fantasize they'd take out Robin's baby book to show me his first giggling photo. We'd cozily drink tea and eat some homemade cookies, then pick out baby names.

Instead, I explain to them that Robin and I have grown apart, that he is away frequently, that he hangs out with his friends and has no time for me. I want to tell them the truth about his friend Mike, but they might not understand, and there is no reason to hurt them.

Finally, his mother says, "Well, you can't just quit."

My mother-in-law is of the generation, like my mother, that believes you stick it out and make your marriage work. But even my mother knows that my marriage is broken. My mother-in-law looks off, saying, resigned, "Well, boys will be boys."

How can she say that? Then inside, I get angry at Robin. *He* is the one who stayed out late, *he* preferred his friend Mike to me. It's *his* fault. But I can't say that to them because what I am telling them is already awful enough.

My mother-in-law finishes the conversation. "We'll see; hopefully things have a way of working out."

The mood is ominous. I get the sense that my in-laws are in shock— and why wouldn't they be? Robin and I never gave them a hint that we were unhappy. We barely talked about our relationship ourselves.

"Marriage can be tough sometimes," my father-in-law says, shifting uncomfortably in his seat. It suddenly occurs to me that he is the minority leader of the United States House of Representatives, a member of Congress for nearly three decades, a World War II Purple Heart and Bronze Star recipient, and *I* am causing him to shift uncomfortably in his seat. *I* am bringing him defeat. *I* am marring his perfect family and leaving a hole in future Christmas cards. Why couldn't I just stay in my place? Robin is not a bad person. He didn't mean to hurt me, I rationalize to myself.

Still, I am unhappy. Deeply unhappy. The unhappiness inside of me has built slowly—nights when I was alone, when Robin was out of town or out with friends. The only person I complained to was my mother who constantly told me "a marriage takes work." And now, as I look at my in-laws and take in their silence, I sadly realize that there is no more work to do on this marriage.

9

Though I remain calm on the exterior for the most part, inside I am a hurricane. I am turbulent and unsteady. At times when I am unable to remain calm on the exterior, my polite, agreeable persona gets invaded by physical manifestations of fear, and I have a panic attack. Right in the middle of my day. I break out in a sweat, my heart beats like a jazz drum, and thoughts of "what if people notice me" race through my mind. I want to escape, but it's impossible.

Now that Robin and I are divorcing, panic attacks are normal. I am fear-filled. It feels as though my sadness has morphed into a kind of despair—an emotional changing of the guard. I've never lived alone before. Will I meet someone else? Should I get a dog? With my fear, there remains, though, a residue of sorrow, so it gives it an extra dimension, as if plain old fear weren't enough.

The physical manifestation of this fear happens on a Monday when I am meeting with Nancy Reynolds in her office. Nancy is her typical, dazzling whirlwind of energy. Her phone rings off the hook, her secretary rushes in and out with messages.

"Now, I want you to take notes for a new client. By the way, Pam, we are delighted you're here!"

I look at her. Everything is fine in this moment. But I feel a panic attack coming out of nowhere. The edges of my mouth tingle. My scalp becomes pins and needles. My throat and my chest tighten. My palms get clammy. I listen as Nancy tells me how she adores my parents. I smile, trying to camouflage my fear. If Nancy knows something is wrong, she doesn't let on. I'm Wick Junior, the supposedly cool, effective, daughter of Charles and Mary Jane. No wonder she feels I was a good hire. But inside I'm falling apart so I can't even operate, because I'm having a panic attack. What I wouldn't give to *not* get a rush of adrenaline as my body feels anxious, as if it can sense an oncoming train. My armpits are sweaty under my silk blouse.

My panic attacks, I imagine, are a business bonanza for my neighborhood dry cleaners. I take my sweaters and blouses almost daily. The owners must wonder why I go through my tops so quickly. Maybe they think I work out in them?

The next day, I'm in a staff meeting. Anne Wexler, another founder of the firm, a former advisor in the Carter administration, sits at the head of a conference table. Tailored jacket, chunky gold earrings—she knows everyone in town. Now she's talking to *me*.

"Pam, the lawyers from the New York Power Authority are coming down from Albany next week. I want you to escort these guys to the Hill. Take copious notes."

And yet again, my nerves set in. How do I get to the Hill? What kind of notes should I take? Wait, what is a power authority?

As I nervously scrawl notes on my pad, I hope that no one notices that my inner hurricane is now a typhoon. Pam Curtis shoots me a supportive glance, which helps me to feel less stressed. *These are nice people, Pam. No one's out to get you*, I tell myself.

I know they don't really have it in for me, but they have such impressive resumes. It's not that they purposely worked hard and got good jobs to make me feel less by comparison. That would be ridiculous, I know. But these are remarkable professionals, "the Top People," as my mother would say. They have been legislative aides, policy analysts for men like Jimmy Carter and Walter Mondale; some are lawyers.

And me? I majored in French poetry and painting in college. I can talk Baudelaire's imagery in *Les Fleurs du mal*, Monet's color and light, and the transgressive and surreal themes of Rimbaud's poetry. But they're not interested in hearing my analysis of art, or the fact that I was a salesgirl at Saks Fifth Avenue, a floating temp at the Art Institute of Chicago, or that I had a job as a gift wrapper in high school. These don't feel like transferable skills. I'm overwhelmed, taking slow, deep breaths to calm myself. *You can do this*, I tell myself, halfheartedly.

10

When I show up at Dad's office to meet him for dinner, I notice how gracefully he manages his work life. Most of his employees have gone home. We stand in his outer office and I watch my father: his dark hair, elegant suit, striped tie. He motions to the large wall clocks set to Moscow, Paris, Brussels, New York, Washington, DC. It feels kind of like a global command center.

"Darling, isn't this fabulous?" he says, brimming with happiness. I can tell he wouldn't want to be anywhere else. He's so unlike me. I would rather be anywhere than at my job.

As director of the United States Information Agency (USIA), the government's multimillion-dollar public relations bureau, my father runs Voice of America, Radio Free Europe, the Fulbright Program, and over 211 USIA posts in over 174 countries. I marvel at how he has made the transition from Hollywood to DC. He wrote and directed a film for 20th Century Fox when we were kids: *Snow White and the Three Stooges*, starring Moe, Larry, and Curly. Snow White was played by the Olympic skating champion Carol Heiss. We used to visit the set at the studio where there was a large skating lake with black ice. We loved walking on it. There, too, Dad was at the center of bustling activity. Maybe he's always been a director at heart. Before he directed the USIA, he directed life.

A large map covers nearly the entire wall, with small lights indicating USIA posts in countries all over the world.

"It's probably an issue with the circuits," says Joe, a grey-haired electrician who has come to repair the map lights, some of which have stopped working. "I'll need to get some replacement fuses."

"Say that again, Joe." My father races to grab his Dictaphone so that he can record Joe's analysis of the situation. "Joe, speak into this machine and I'll have my secretary type it up. Next time there's a problem, we'll have a record of what went wrong this time." Instead of taking notes, my father records what everyone says. I'm not sure whether this is the best time-saving method ever or simply one of my father's numerous idiosyncrasies.

When my siblings and I were young, Dad would routinely record every electrician who came to our house to repair the stereo, every film technician who came to repair our screening projector, even our swimming teacher Miss Finny, who once spent ten minutes describing how to do the backstroke—"Pam, your shoulders need to rotate with your hands!"—my father standing next to her with his Dictaphone, she in her large sunhat and dripping in suntan lotion.

Our father loved cameras as well. He took photos of every birthday, Christmas, and Easter with his Nikon, directing us to stand at certain angles as he held his light meter to our faces.

"Isn't this fabulous?" my father says, motioning to the giant map where Joe is still working. As usual, Dad waves his arms in a grand gesture. He is always larger than life.

I think about the hundreds of people throughout the world who are posted where those lights are placed on the map. It would be daylight in many of those places now. Even though it is night here and Dad is in his office, his employees are listening to him through memos and directives overseas. What must it feel like to radiate that kind of influence? I have no idea.

Two hours later, we are in a booth at The Palm Restaurant. I am desperate to tell him what is really happening with me, with my job. I want him to assuage my fears about how I feel unqualified.

Normally my father is a good listener. He leans forward, looks you in the eye, his head nods with understanding, and he makes you feel that you have all the time in the world to talk. Tonight, though, is not a good time. Tonight, "It's showtime." My father has used this expression throughout our lives. This is code for be ready, look your best, and be prepared to be "on." He used it before our birthday parties, when the guests were about to arrive, the balloons tied to the front door, the birthday cake set out. When we heard him say this, we somehow felt important, as if we were the entertainment. It was exciting. He even used it before my wedding, just as he was about to walk me down the aisle. Standing at the entrance to the church, I clutched my bouquet, waiting for our cue to walk forward. My father turned to me, lovingly looked me in the eye, and said, "Darling, it's showtime." He used this expression before President and Mrs. R would arrive at our home in Washington for our annual Christmas Eve celebrations. As the presidential motorcade would be about to pull into our driveway, our father would move through the house, in his velvet pants, poking his head into our rooms as we'd scramble to be ready, "Come on guys, it's showtime!" I think the expression comes from his producing days in Hollywood with the Tommy Dorsey Band.

The room is filled with senators, congressmen, lobbyists, important people. And we need to be "on." My parents have only been here for a couple of years, but it seems like Dad already knows everyone in Washington. Before we even receive our salad course, he has spotted Bob Dole, the Republican senator from Kansas.

Without another word Dad jumps up from the table and makes a beeline for Dole's table. I watch from across the room. My father is leaning over Dole's table, talking to the senator and another man. All of a sudden, the men burst into laughter. Dole wipes away tears, he is laughing so hard. I know why. Dad no doubt told a joke. He has a mental catalogue of jokes he springs on the most unsuspecting person. His current favorite is: "Did you hear about the guy who was half Jewish and half Japanese? Every December 7th he would bomb Pearl Schwartz!"

As my father returns to our table, he appears energized by his encounter. "What a guy, Senator Dole. He's accomplished a hell of a lot."

I know that tomorrow my father will write a personal note to the senator, telling him he enjoyed seeing him at The Palm. Then, in the future, if there is any further business with the Senate Finance Committee, Dad will easily reach Bob Dole. I have learned that this is the way things work in Washington, and no one is better at this than my father. Tonight, I know he must feel so proud of himself.

* * *

I REALIZE MY FATHER HAS WANTED THIS LIFE, this important and powerful life, since he was young. Growing up, he always told us how difficult it was for him. He grew up in a small house in Cleveland with his Russian Jewish immigrant parents, who couldn't afford to pay for his education. They did manage to buy Dad a used piano, recognizing his musical talent. (He has something called "perfect pitch," where he can identify any musical note just by hearing it.) He worked his way through college and then law school by forming a jazz band and performing for student dances. In the summer he played at the Grand Hotel on Mackinac Island in Michigan. The wealthy from Detroit, Chicago, and other cities danced under the stars, enjoying cocktails on the Grand Hotel's six-hundred-foot veranda overlooking a vast tea garden and the straits of Mackinac.

"My folks couldn't believe it," he'd tell us growing up, recalling how he loved to write home to his parents to describe the lobster, the caviar, the expensive clothing worn by guests, the grandeur of being in such a place. President Harry Truman stayed at the hotel, as well as Thomas

Edison and other high-profile business leaders. This was American aristocracy.

One day, someone referred to him as "Jew boy." Dad had encountered anti-Semitism in the past, but this particular instance cut through him, as though he was "spotted." It decimated him.

Eventually he fought back. He was determined to fit seamlessly into high society. He bought books on manners, taught himself how to use a soupspoon, learned the right fork for salads, took diction lessons and practiced enunciating his words with eloquence, and finally changed his name from Charles Zwick to Charles Z. Wick. Later, he married our mother, a beautiful, blonde Grace Kelly lookalike, a John Robert Powers model, the daughter of a struggling single mother from Minnesota. Mom's ambitions matched those of my father's. They were determined to build a life of prestige.

11

The Cannon House Office Building, an imposing marble and limestone Beaux-Arts building, is located south of the US Capitol on Independence Avenue. As I escort the two attorneys from the New York Power Authority up the steep concrete steps, I gaze up at the vast marble columns, the fall sunlight casting a silvery tone. It seems that in Washington I always feel small, and this moment is no exception. Even my professional outfit, a houndstooth jacket and matching flared skirt, pales in comparison to the enormity and importance of this building and this town.

As we wait in the lobby of Congressman Solarz's office, Vince, a serious-looking guy, asks me a question about an energy subcommittee that is holding hearings next week, and I realize that I have no idea what he is talking about: FERC? I hesitate, trying to come up with the answer. Then I freeze. Why can't he just say the words? Why does everyone do this? I rack my brain. Federal, Energy...my heart starts to beat fast and I feel like I'm breaking out in a cold sweat. I look at my spiral notebook where I have prepared a cheat sheet. In big letters I have written FERC; I *know* what this means, but I'm so nervous I blanked. Inside my tote bag I also have flash cards with terms I need to know. "Hydropower," or harnessing electricity from water, is on my first flash card—that's not hard, I think to myself.

In my anxiety a question suddenly poses itself: Why am I here? In Washington. In this building. I have no interest. Not that I don't think it's important, and not that I don't respect these guys for their work. But the only thing that excites me about being here is the drama and majesty of this building. And the paintings lining the hallways. I don't have an answer as to why I'm here except that I followed Robin.

Before I know it, we're in the meeting. Joe and Vince take turns pitching the economic benefits of their power line project to the congressional staffer, a small, preppy man with glasses who makes notes on his legal pad. I desperately try to capture the conversation on my notepad. But I'm overwhelmed by the acronyms, and physical geography of New York State, and the names of congressional committees. Is Rochester north or south of Syracuse? Does the power line cross Westchester?

I take some flash cards out of my tote, then I pull out my geography cheat sheet. The power line does not cross Westchester. That's good. I know that. Joe looks over at me, as if he wishes I'd stop doing this, like I am annoying him, with all the paper and flash card shuffling, so I stop. I look at my watch. We have been sitting in the windowless office for forty minutes.

Finally, back outside, we head toward the steep bank of concrete steps, which lead down to Independence Avenue. Vince says something that tells me they are pleased with the meeting. I am relieved—it's over, and it went well, even though I didn't make much of a contribution, but I did try looking at my notes.

"Cheap hydropower, who can argue with that?" I say, cheerfully, hoping talking shop will get me new friends.

Joe looks over at me and says sarcastically, "Oh, I don't know. Maybe the grain farmer who doesn't want his land taken away so a giant hydroelectric generator line can be built, worried his family will be exposed to radiation and get cancer and he'll lose his dream of a good life."

I was just trying to lighten the mood, and I realize that I've stuck my foot in it.

And then as if life were trying to parody my thought, I literally stick my foot in it. As I take a step down one of the concrete steps, the front part of my shoe slips into a crack. Before I can process what has happened, I'm off balance, my body lurching forward.

My legs are suddenly apart like I am about to do the splits. I try to regain my balance by throwing my arms up, which entails letting go of my folder. Flash cards soar into the air. The contents of my tote spill out. I land with a thud; my shoe flies out in front of me. I see flash cards scattered on the steps in front of me, two regular-size tampons that have fallen out of my tote, and my bright pink hairbrush that has rolled down five steps.

Vince and Joe rush toward me as they scramble to pick up the flash cards. They lean down, handing me my tote. I reach out to grab the tampons. They turn their heads as if they are embarrassed to see my feminine hygiene products.

Both men appear worried. Joe's eyebrows knit together as he searches my face as I wince in pain. Vince takes hold of my arm, as if to make sure it's not broken.

"Are you okay?" they ask in unison.

"I'm fine, I'm good," I say, wishing I were somewhere else as I grab my hairbrush. I can't stand up at the moment; I'm dizzy, so both men, noticing this, sit down next to me on the enormous bank of concrete stairs. It's such an awkward moment; no one knows what to say. I get the sense that the guys feel sorry for me. Joe clears his throat, filling the silence, as I slowly stuff some papers back in my tote. They are now suddenly like big brothers, kind of protective, on either side of me.

"Take all the time you need," says Joe.

He has morphed from a Brooklyn tough guy to a mama's boy, and Vince has changed from a dry, electrical-industry attorney to a soft, concerned human. It is a rare and treasured moment of authenticity, and yet I can't even appreciate the moment through my distress. I feel utterly imperfect.

12

President Reagan's diary entry from December 24, 1983: *Tis the day before Christmas & all thru the house—yes there is a bustle. Ron & Doria arrive from N.Y. for lunch. Patti & her friend Paul Grilley will be in late. Christmas Eve dinner at the Wicks is beginning to be a tradition. One cloud in the sky. I'll keep to myself—the threat world wide by the Iranian fanatics to loose terror on everything American. The Wicks dinner was as always, a warm, wonderful time with long time friends. I played Santa Claus—another part of the tradition but my 1st time to play the role.*

Ronald Reagan will look back fondly on the Christmas of 1983 with our family. Mrs. R will remind us about the turkey that year, how my mother got the stuffing just right, how we convinced the president to play Santa. But that Christmas will always hold a different meaning for me. It will always be the season that everything changed. That Christmas was the calm before the storm, before our world turned upside down. None of us, though, saw a storm on the horizon, not a single grey cloud in the sky. We assumed our perfect life would continue, its high-octane wonderfulness rolled out each day before us. The only one who was under a cloud was me. But that had nothing to do with what was to come.

It's Christmas Eve, and I am having a hard time getting into the spirit. It's not just that my parents moved the tradition from Los

Angeles to Washington. It's a mix of everything—my divorce, my job... or perhaps maybe it's just a premonition.

My sisters and brothers, on the other hand, don't sense anything wrong. They are filled with holiday cheer. They have flown in from other cities and everyone is getting ready for our annual Christmas Eve celebration.

As I step toward the door of my room, dressed in velvet, patting down my teased and sprayed hair, I hear the sound of my sisters' voices coming from my bathroom.

"You're going to break it!" Kim says, wrestling the blow-dryer from Cindy, who's just out of the shower.

Cindy laughs as she towels off her own hair and teases Kim, "You're wearing black pants tonight? B-o-r-i-n-g!"

As I watch them getting ready, I think about how my sisters are living their best twenty-something lives. They are adventurous and courageous—Kim has just returned to California after a year in Australia. Like Cindy, she too escaped all the pressures of leading a domestic life.

My sisters stay out late, work hard, get hangovers on the weekend—everything I didn't get to experience. With the ink barely dry on my college diploma I trotted down the aisle on my father's arm into the arms of my husband.

Watching them get ready, I feel uncertain and adrift. Cindy brushes her hair in rhythmic strokes, appearing so purposeful, as if in the simple act of grooming she takes full ownership over herself. There is no hesitation, no wondering, "Is this how I'm supposed to wear my hair?" For me, it's as if there's a committee in my head I must consult each time I exhale.

This committee is made up of my parents—and even different versions of them. There is my nice mother, my discerning mother, my controlling mother, my empathetic mother. And then there are several versions of my father: the generous one, the volatile one, the caring one, the critical one. They all live in my head; they all have an opinion.

Let's say when I come home with a new dress, all of the committee members chime in.

My discerning mother: It doesn't show off your waist enough.

My controlling mother: I should have gone shopping with you. This is a mistake.

My funny father: On sale means you wind up paying more.

My volatile father: What the hell? Your mother knows fashion. Why didn't you ask her first?

It is noisy in my head as they argue and finally vote on what I should buy next time. It happens for every decision I make.

Now I look over at Cindy, confident in everything that she does. There is no committee in her head. Just my sister deciding what to wear, whom to date, what color to paint her kitchen (it's bright turquoise at the moment). She's younger than I. Why is she so good at making decisions without hesitating?

Almost as if reading my mind, she says, "You were the first girl; Mom poured everything into you."

Maybe it is as simple as that. It's not that I am all that different from my sisters. It's simply that I came before them. But I wonder, was being the oldest really the only reason that we turned out so different?

My mother has often told me how excited she and my father were when I was born. "Finally, a girl." As if she was waiting to have someone like herself, someone she could recognize, and on whom she could pin her hopes and dreams. Which is probably where the problem began. I imagine my birth, taking my first breath, my mother gazing into my eyes and breathing along with me. But soon, it was as if she was breathing for me. It was as if even my birth was made for teamwork. I was never to be alone, but be part of something larger than myself.

Growing up, I kept up my end of my birth bargain. I said the right thing, did the right thing. I read my parents' faces, and when they smiled, it meant they approved of me. If I disappointed, they could be fierce, my father with his fiery temper. His anger scared me.

Once, when I was five, he found that someone had removed his stapler from his study. He started yelling our names, and "Which one of you kids took my stapler from my desk?"

I didn't know who had taken the stapler; it wasn't me, but I wanted to be out of range of his piercing voice reverberating through the house. I ran into the dining room and hid under the antique polished-wood dining chair with calming floral upholstery. There I stayed, safe from his anger. I did this over the years every time I felt afraid and needed to feel safe.

Along with my father's anger my mother could have an icy detachment. She would withdraw her warmth until I did what she wanted. I felt left in the cold until she reconnected with me. This kept me working hard for their approval. I needed so badly to hear their encouraging words: "You are good"; "You look beautiful in that dress"; "You got straight A's; your father and I are so proud of you."

So, rather than reaching inside myself to ask, *What do you want?* I reached outside to ask, what do *they* want? And I've done this for so long that I no longer know what I want. It's become a habit to look outside myself for answers. Which means I no longer even know who I am.

I watch my sister, and I'm filled with love for her, but also with amazement: She has the freedom to be imperfect, a luxury I never had. She can be volatile like Dad, shouting back at him in a way I never did. And she can be impulsive. She once decided to go parachuting out of a plane before attending one of my parents' dinner parties. She is not wearing velvet tonight on Christmas Eve; instead, she is stepping into crinkled, gauzy flea-market pants. She is her own person.

An hour later, any illusion that this is a normal holiday season filled with Christmas cheer has disappeared. Now Secret Service agents are posted around the perimeter of the house, sharp shooters are on the roof, and the interior of the house has been "swept"—a term for a deep security check. Even the drapes are drawn over the large, floor-to-ceiling windows throughout the house to protect President Reagan from view. I listen as two Secret Service men talk into their walkie-talkies, monitoring the presidential motorcade en route to our house. "Rawhide northeast corner, approaching driveway, headed for garage entry." It feels serious and even ominous.

Moments later the presidential limousine bearing flags on the front pulls into the garage and comes to a halt. The agents jump to the passenger doors. President Reagan and Mrs. R step out of the car and walk through the side door into the kitchen. Behind them follow Ron and his wife Doria, and Patti and her boyfriend Paul. The entourage is accompanied by a military aide carrying a briefcase, or, as it is called, the nuclear football. The black leather bag contains the nuclear codes to authorize an attack while President Reagan is away from the White House. As President and Mrs. R enter our house, I sense something behind their eyes, a weighted quality, a heaviness I've never noticed. Even though they are smiling, it's as if they are burdened by the threats that surround them.

I understand the need for security, even if I still haven't gotten used to the fact that the man who once told stories in our living room is now the actual president of the United States. But it makes me long for the Christmases past when the Reagans would drive themselves to our house, sometimes in their station wagon, and walk up to our front door carrying Christmas gifts—no security, no threats. We'd open the door and greet them, and our Norman Rockwell evening would begin. I want tonight to be like old times. I want the Secret Service, the briefcase with the nuclear codes to go away. I want my mother and Mrs. R to be in checked aprons making chili at our school fair. I need it to be like old times, when I wasn't overwhelmed by my job, my life—when everything felt so simple. I fall back into feeling uncertain and adrift, as I watch the Reagans carry the weight of the world on their shoulders.

Later, I try to appear upbeat against the dazzling Christmas tree as we have drinks. Ron Jr. is living with his wife Doria in New York, and Patti flew in from Los Angeles. Ron, who has always known how to make me laugh, gives me a hug. I can tell he feels sad for me. No jokes tonight. He has the kindest expression on his face. Patti then comes over and takes my hand sympathetically. "Divorce... So tough, Pam."

In spite of Ron and Patti's comforting words, I still feel upside down. I watch Mrs. R in her crepe blouse, sipping a white wine, standing with my mother and brothers. She glances over at me with a reassuring smile, as if reading my thoughts. I want this to make me feel better, but it doesn't. I watch my siblings delighting in their experience. My oldest brother C.Z., a TV executive in Los Angeles, teases Mrs. R about him and Patti getting in trouble in fifth grade and her having difficulty punishing them. "There you were, off on your bikes, telling me you had finished your homework!" Mrs. R shakes her head in feigned disapproval.

A touch of panic hits me. I feel so far away, as though I am breathing different air than everyone else in the room. They are having Christmas and I'm not. And I am angry at myself for not being able to fix this. I listen to their voices, so free and joyful, which increases my discomfort. My brother Doug, an aspiring movie producer in New York, jokes with Mrs. R about the chili she and Mom claimed as their own when they ran the chili booth at our school in Los Angeles's annual fair.

"I'm not so sure it was really homemade," laughs Doug.

My mother quickly corrects him. "Doug, it tasted like Chasen's, but it was *our* recipe."

Chasen's was a famous restaurant in Los Angeles loved by celebrities; my parents and the Reagans were loyal patrons. Chasen's chili was so beloved that Elizabeth Taylor had it flown to Rome twice a week while filming *Cleopatra*.

Everyone around me is acting like old times. It's as if they don't care about the Secret Service posted around the house, the sharpshooters on the roof. Why can't I simply join the party?

My brothers call Mrs. R "double o," short for 007, a nickname they gave her since she routinely sleuths information about Ron and Patti from them. She blindsides them with questions such as "How is Ron doing? Is he alright?" "I haven't heard from Patti." My brothers typically respond cryptically. "Patti's fine," which means she spent the night with her boyfriend. Or, "Ron stayed up late working," which means he's still asleep on our couch.

"Double o, why don't you play Santa this year," my brother C.Z. now suggests to Mrs. R. We are drinking eggnog in front of a sparkling Christmas tree, a roaring fire in the fireplace.

Besides the music, the apple pies, and Mrs. R and Mom's monkey bread, there is always Santa Claus. Each year someone plays the role and dresses in the family Santa suit.

"I can't play Santa," Mrs. R says to my brother. "I wouldn't take that away from the president." A few Christmases later Mrs. R will indeed play Santa; we will place three calls to Ron Jr. in California at the time, to convince her to accept the role. Mrs. R, a good sport, will allow us to stuff extra pillows to help her fill out the extra-large costume.

"That's my job," President Reagan says, overhearing us, grinning in anticipation.

How do you dress the president of the United States as Santa Claus? I think about this as I follow Ronald Reagan, my mother, and my siblings into the back bedroom where the red-and-white costume is laid out on the bed. Mom brings in a tray of makeup and places it on the night-stand. My brothers, sisters, and I assist. President Reagan sits at the edge of the bed and pulls the giant red pants with black vinyl belt over his dress slacks. Mom starts applying blush to his cheeks.

"Mary Jane," President Reagan jokes, "that's my color."

"Hold still or I'll powder your eye!"

Now I am finally at peace. A soft, relaxed feeling engulfs me. We are back in Los Angeles, and it is Christmas Eve. The house is filled with red-bowed garlands; pine smells mix with night-blooming jasmine. The make-believe Hollywood of my childhood. Ronald Reagan is in ward-robe, hair, and makeup, as he used to be. He has lost the burdened, weighty appearance behind his eyes. He is not worried about Lebanon or Iran. Rather, he is laughing with something that resembles a childlike joy, a complete lack of trepidation.

Probably because he doesn't know what's about to happen to my family. None of us yet do on this cheery Christmas day.

13

It's the morning after Christmas and I am feeling peaceful. The stereo is playing throughout the house, my father is laughing with my siblings in the living room, and I made it through my first Christmas without Robin. Even the anxiety over my job feels far away.

"Honey, the phone is for you," my mother calls to me.

I hesitate for an instant; is it Robin, wishing me a Merry Christmas?

"Post-Christmas sale at Garfinckel's? Want to go?"

It's Pam Curtis from work. Her voice is enthusiastic and warm and it's totally unexpected. I think about when I met her for the first time: I was a wreck that day in the office, but I had felt a connection. I'm glad to hear her voice now.

Glancing around the room, I watch my family fighting over a See's candy box and realize that when I return, they will probably still be right here, in front of the fireplace, in sugar comas. I'm not missing anything.

I arrive at Garfinckel's, *the* department store in downtown DC. It is a 1920s elaborate, imposing building, and it feels like shopping here is important, somehow. As I think about it, all buildings in Washington are important—the Capitol, the Supreme Court Building, the Library of Congress. So why should a department store be any different? Garfinckel's is where people buy important clothes to attend important events and important meetings. Government affairs is serious business.

The sidewalk is packed with shoppers waiting for the doors to open. I spot Pam bundled in a puffer coat and cashmere scarf looking utterly chic. How does she manage to look *so* fabulous both in and out of the office? Then again, this is Washington. I have on my "good cloth" coat, a hat, and loafers. My feet are freezing, but I'm happy. And freezing is not even the worst feeling I've ever experienced.

"You made it," Pam smiles at me.

This feels like a real outing with a friend. I haven't yet made any friends here. I miss my girlfriends in California, the laughter, the closeness. I call them long distance, watching the minutes tick by as the phone bill gets huge.

We step inside Garfinckel's; the air is sweet and musky as we walk by the perfume counters. Pam stops suddenly. She spritzes "Charlie" on her wrist, a hyacinth, lily-of-the-valley scent. "My favorite," she announces. I notice the ad featuring a young working woman, dashing down a city street, carefree, and confident. The caption reads, *"Charlie. When you're living in the fast lane."*

I imagine me on a cold, grey Washington day, independent and purposeful, like that girl in the Charlie ad, dressed in flowy pants and heels. It's such a contrast to what I'm wearing now. I look at my loafers and button-down shirt and I wonder to myself, *When did I start dressing like a man?* Was it when Robin and I moved to Chicago? When I was working as a temporary secretary at the Art Institute, I had started picking out what I considered "serious" work clothes.

It feels normal to me to not be colorful and stand out, especially when in meetings with mostly men in Washington. As a woman, you are already different, so isn't it better to fit in, in order to be taken seriously? As if reading my thoughts, Pam says, "Just because we fight for equal rights doesn't mean we dress like men."

I like Pam's advice about clothes and about life. She is so confident and has a way of expressing her views that inspire me. As she holds up a silk jersey Diane Von Furstenberg wrap dress with a tiny, colorful logo print, my heart skips a beat. "Throw on that wrap dress and feel like a million bucks," Pam says. Is it that easy? To feel like a million bucks? I can reignite my fearful self and *feel* a new, better way? Maybe. It's as if I have the power to change my insides with my outsides, and Pam is my cheerleader.

Exhausted by all the shopping, we finally haul our overfull bags down to the department store restaurant. Pam feels like an older sister. "You get to wear clothes that excite you. *You* get to choose," she encourages me.

The wrap dress is my favorite purchase. The silk jersey cinches at the waist and the skirt drapes perfectly; I think it makes me look like Audrey Hepburn.

We take a seat at an upholstered booth of floral fabric surrounded by trellis with greenery. The Greenbrier, she tells me, is her happy place. My happy place is Will Wright's in Westwood Village, with its pink-and-white striped awnings and peppermint stick ice cream. But now, I am content to sit here, listening to the chatter of shoppers as Pam and I peruse the menu.

I look at Pam and notice her soft blue eyes, mascara slightly smudged, the effect making her seem kind of imperfect. I feel comfortable confiding in her. I tell her that I'm scared at work, about my general fear of not knowing enough. Pam says it's natural, that I'm new at my job and it takes time.

"Aren't you ever afraid, even now?" I ask her. Pam has been working in politics for years.

Pam considers my question, then starts to answer.

"Listen, the greatest leaders, Kennedy, Martin Luther King, the Pope, have fear now and had fear then. They're human. But you just forge ahead."

I try and take this in, but the idea that I could forge ahead like Kennedy in a crisis feels a little too overwhelming.

14

There are moments where everything changes. Something happens and you are caught by surprise. The emotional shock can transform itself into something physical, literally knocking you to the ground. The blow can be so fierce that you are left totally disoriented for months, even years. For me this happens on the day after Christmas, as I return to my parents' house after my shopping trip with Pam.

As I walk in the front, loaded down with Garfinckel's bags, I am met with an eerie silence. The Christmas music, playing when I left this morning, is off. My mother always insists on ringing in the New Year with "Hark! The Herald Angel Sings," but now there are no cheery carols, not even the sound of conversation.

"Is anyone home?"

Cody the Doberman meanders down the hallway to greet me. Too distracted to give him the head pats he's craving, I glance inside the living room. It is empty, but I notice a silver tray with coffee and cookies on the center table.

"Hello?!" I yell through the house. All I hear is the echo of my own voice. Where is everyone? No one goes out the day after Christmas. Everyone sits around the tree, where I left them, eating leftovers, watching football, my mother throwing out wrapping paper. Scenarios play out in my head: They are next door visiting neighbors; they went for a walk after too many See's candies and leftovers. I imagine my father saying to my mother, "no more See's, I need to cut back" as he shoves another caramel buttercream into his mouth, suggesting they go for a walk. But then, why wouldn't they have taken the dog if they went walking?

Then I start to fear: They're kidnapped or killed. So *where* is my family?

I continue down the hallway to my parents' bedroom. When I reach their door, I hear voices inside. I try to open the door but it is locked. This throws me. Is my family being held hostage? My parents joke about my father being a target of the Russians; my father finds the Kremlin intrigue comical for some reason. I knock on the door, yelling, "What's going on?" There is no answer; my panic accelerates from zero to sixty. I bang on the door.

My father yells from behind the closed door, "Honey, we're not ready to talk about this and involve you."

So, they're alive. Thank God.

"So, when are you going to let me in?"

No reply.

"Dad, why can't you talk to me?"

"I don't think you should know," my father says through the door. "In case you're called to testify."

I can't believe what I am hearing. Legal scenarios fill my head; I imagine being on the witness stand. "Testify" under oath implies a crime. What is the crime?

When my father finally opens the door, I can tell that my mother has been crying. She is seated. My brothers stare somberly at the floor.

I try to follow what my father is saying but the words boomerang in my head, "punishable," "illegal," "prison." Then I get a pit in my stomach as I experience the gravity of what I am hearing. Freedom of Information Act. Act of Congress? It sounds so ominous.

I look at my father as he is talking to me. He is serious and angry at the same time, then resignation overcomes him. He lowers his head, suddenly deflated and small-looking. I feel dread as I watch him morph into a lesser version of himself.

"I taped telephone calls."

"To whom?" I ask.

Dad looks at me and doesn't say a word. Then...

"Cabinet secretaries. Congressmen. Some others."

The room is silent. My mother and brothers don't say a word.

I already know that my father records everyone. Joe the electrician was his latest subject. But I've never thought anything of it.

"Do other people tape in DC? Is it normal?"

"Honey. Frankly, I didn't think about it. It was routine."

My mother rushes to his defense as she always does.

"He's a stickler for detail. He wants to get it all down."

The problem, as my father explains it, is it's illegal to tape people without informing them. But my father was only doing this to have an accurate record of the conversations for follow up, he explains.

Worse is the fact that all of this is about to come out in the *New York Times*. William Safire's article on my father is slated to be published the next day.

"So that's why William Safire came over this morning?"

My father nods. I had spotted the journalist arriving as I was leaving. I knew my father had a *New York Times* interview.

In this moment, I am mostly confused. I don't quite understand the repercussions. Will Dad get to keep his job? Will he go to prison? What will happen to me at work? How can I go back to the office? At least the worst has already happened, I think to myself.

On December 27, 1983, William Safire's article is on the front page of the *New York Times*: "U.S.I.A Director Acknowledges Taping Telephone Calls in Secret."

15

But the next day is a media frenzy. I learn this when I step out of the house to drive to the grocery store. I get into my mother's black Cadillac Eldorado in the garage, then click the remote to open the garage door. As I slowly back out into the snowy driveway, I notice through my rearview window a lone figure standing. As I get closer, I realize it's a man, scruffy in jeans and parka, pointing a long-focus-lens camera at our house. Suddenly a second guy in a knit cap, also clutching a camera, jumps out of the snow-covered bushes. *Oh, my God!* I can't believe what I'm seeing. This must be about my father! How can they do this? They are trespassing!

My parents' driveway is maybe fifty feet long and descends slightly onto Rock Creek Drive. Both cameramen are now blocking my exit to the street. I can see the first cameraman has a mustache. He is taking pictures of my mother's car, with *me* inside.

I yell to him through my rolled-up car windows, "Get out!" But he can't hear me, so he steps closer. I back the car up slightly again, hoping he'll move. He continues snapping photos. The other cameraman is taking wide-angle photos of the house. They don't actually care about *me*. They just want their shots. If I accidentally opened my door and fell out of the car while moving backward, they'd probably just keep taking pictures while I lay in the snow, as my mother's car plowed into the bushes or rolled into the street. The injustice of my current situation fuels my rage. I step on the gas. The car flies backward. The mustached cameraman dives into the bushes. The second guy dodges the car by a few inches, tossing his camera into the snow. I peel out of the driveway.

Moments later, I screech to a stop on Rock Creek Drive, trying to calm myself. My hands are shaking, holding onto the steering wheel. I can see my breath inside the car, it's so cold. I replay the scene in my mind. *Did I injure one of these guys? I hope they are okay.* Then I curse them for being in our driveway and for trespassing. I fight off a panic attack, wondering how these guys know where we live. Are there more of them? Will they be here every day?

After a quick stop at the grocery store, I arrive back at my parents' house, nervously pulling into the driveway. I can't believe it; there are more cameramen. They are perched in the snow, aiming their long lenses at our house. They see me driving in and turn their cameras toward the car. I struggle to go back into the driveway, glaring at them through my window because my voice is hoarse from yelling earlier. I somehow pull into the garage and click the remote to shut the door behind the car, and I enter the house through the kitchen, shaking. My mother is waiting for me. She, too, appears shaken. "Pamela!" That's what she calls me when she is upset.

"Listen, we got a call from ABC News," my mother continues.

My heart stops. This actually gets worse?

"They claimed *I* tried to run over a cameraman." She is frantic. "What *were* you doing?" Her eyes bore through me.

I am mad all of a sudden. How can she even say that?

"I didn't try to run over those guys. What are you talking about? There was a driveway full of reporters. I was backing out."

Mom looks scared as she stands in the kitchen, her cheerful yellow dishtowels from California hanging neatly behind her. I feel a great foreboding. It no longer seems safe in our own house, so unlike our home in California, which always felt safe. On Sunday mornings, my mother always made waffles with her trusty waffle iron, and fresh squeezed orange juice. We read the funnies in the newspaper and our father told jokes around the breakfast table. But here in Washington, things are changing, and changing fast. I look back at my mother. Are we going to be okay? Will Dad be okay? What will happen? She always knows what to do.

All of a sudden, Mom shifts. Rather than reassure me, she shuts down. She's done. I watch as she goes into survival mode. She nervously checks to make sure the kitchen door is locked, then begins unloading the dishwasher. Methodically, in a sort of zombie-like way, she picks up plates and stacks them in the cabinet above. *Clink, clink*—the china hits the shelf. Then, as if it is not even the same day, she starts to ask me if we should have leftover ham for dinner, with tomato soup. As if we can pretend none of the bad stuff has happened, and none of the bad stuff lies ahead of us. As I watch her, it occurs to me that this is the first time I've seen her scared, and a knot inside my stomach tightens. The irony of the entire last twenty-four hours, the difficulty and unanswered questions...it feels like I am drowning in a sea of doubt and fear.

16

A day later, it is bitter cold. Snow on the ground, icicles dangling from tree branches—a Currier-and-Ives winter scene. The exterior of our house still looks Christmassy, holly berries in big pots flanking the modern entryway.

"My turn next!" my sister Kim says. She presses the button on the garage door opener. As the door rises, several reporters and cameramen, parked at the edge of our property, pile out of their cars. They feverishly grab their cameras, desperate to get *the* shot—one of the Wicks, maybe Mrs. Wick, Nancy Reagan's best friend, would be good. Their long lenses point at the garage expectantly.

"Okay, now," shouts Cindy. Kim presses the button again, and the door slowly closes. "False alarm, morons!" shouts Cindy, and we all buckle over in laughter.

My sisters and I have been playing this game for hours. On Cindy's turn, she actually gets into my mother's car, starts the engine, and slowly backs out of the garage, a few feet. Then, she waits. The cameramen literally run up our long driveway, their breath visible in the bitter cold. Cindy then quickly pulls back into the garage, lowering the garage door. The men rush back into their cars, frustrated, bundled in heavy jackets.

Our torture of the paparazzi is intentional. We have made this into a game, a joke, but inside we are furious. They are bottom-feeders, in our view, whose job it is to expose anyone in the news for a buck. Dad's face is plastered all over the place. He is the lead story on the seven o'clock news, the big front-page scoop. These guys are harassing him and will do anything to get a picture.

We are also defending our father. He is our biggest champion and always has been. We love him. And we want this to go away. Since we are otherwise impotent, this game of cat and mouse with the garage door is a prime weapon in our arsenal. Propelled by our anger, we are obsessed with fighting back.

I am a full participant in this activity. My typical "Should we be doing this?" has been replaced with "Goddammit, I don't have to be the good girl." The committee in my head is silent. I am not seeking permission or weighing the opinions of its members, namely my parents, on what I should or should not do. I am joining my sisters in this fight, and maybe for the first time, I am not the sibling who got married and overnight morphed into a hostess with twelve place settings of china and no voice. It feels surprisingly empowering to express my anger. My insides feel energized; I feel purposeful. And my fear, the gateway to my panic attacks, is momentarily lessened.

17

Two hours later, we decide to help our father in another way, our sense of family togetherness solidified. At the request of my father and his attorney, we are organizing Dad's cassette tapes, also known as "the incriminating evidence." Our job is to alphabetize and place them in boxes.

Since we are paranoid that the press will take photos with their Nikon lenses through the windows of our house, Cindy and Kim and I take the tapes and carry them into our mother's dressing room, where empty shoeboxes are stacked. I look around the dressing room as we dump the tapes on the floor. It is a space about twenty by twenty feet, carpeted, and I am relieved that there are no windows.

We sit on the floor of the dressing room, dutifully sorting the tapes and transferring them into shoeboxes. I feel a mixture of purpose and anger. It feels good to be working alongside my sisters and helping our father. My sisters and I are angry at the journalists and the paparazzi who we feel are stalking Dad. In our view, our father is an earnest guy, who was diligently doing his job. Sure, he shouldn't have taped phone conversations without informing the other party, but he wasn't doing this to blackmail anyone. He's just meticulous and had bad judgment. Besides, taping conversations is common practice here in DC. I don't understand why my father is being singled out.

"Jimmy Carter?" Kim hands a cassette to Cindy.

"No. Put him back with the C's."

"You told me to put him with the P's!" Kim barks.

"'P' for president. I didn't mean to *put* him with the P's; I was just talking to myself." Cindy says.

"Casper Weinberger, Secretary of Defense?" Kim asks Cindy like she's the one who's taken it upon herself who decides what goes where and we're merely following her orders.

"Put him under W. We're going by last name." Cindy thinks about this for a moment. "Except for William Safire. He's in a category all by himself. I'd put him under 'A' for asshole."

My sisters and I crack up. William Safire is not actually on any of the cassette tapes.

"Fuck Safire," Cindy says. "He ruins families. Who's the *real* liar here?"

She is holding a cassette tape in her hand. But instead of handing me the tape to put in a shoebox, Cindy, with her pinky finger, begins pulling the tape from its plastic cassette case. Yards of tape unspool as Kim and I watch in horror and amazement.

"Yeah, we're going to help Dad. But for real." Cindy picks up an armful of tapes and starts to walk out of the dressing room into the large master bedroom. "Grab more, follow me."

I feel a sense of dread. As if I am a child doing something wrong. I desperately want to stop my sister.

Cindy reads my horrified face as I look over at the roaring fire in the fireplace, realizing what she is about to do.

"What's the big deal?"

Kim and I are speechless.

Cindy breaks the cassette in two, yanks out the tape, and flings it into the fireplace. We watch as the cassette is swallowed by flames.

Dire scenarios fill my head. "You don't live in DC. The day after tomorrow you will go back to New York and Kim to LA, and *I* will be here, probably getting indicted for destroying evidence, and get fired from my job."

"It's not all about you," Cindy says. "How can you not care about helping Dad?"

I hesitate for a moment, I think about it, and anger erupts inside of me. *This* is our chance to do this, to fight back. We will disrupt the chain of events that the asshole Safire has put into motion! I rev from zero to sixty in a minute.

Half an hour later, we have tossed dozens of tapes into their funeral pyres. Our eyes water from the stench of burning plastic. But given our momentum, we ignore the minor discomfort.

Kim stares wildly into to the fireplace.

"Bye Jimmy Carter, bye Casper Weinberger!" Cindy screams.

We watch as the flames lick the small cassettes. I am awed by our ability to cause such destruction; my adrenaline is pumping; I am rising over the failure of my life and pummeling Safire and everything bad that has happened to our family.

"Woo-hoo!" Cindy says. Kim follows, cheering loudly.

I let out a cheer of my own, surprising myself by the intensity of my voice. I laugh, then toss in a cassette, watching as it is devoured by roaring flames.

* * *

WE LATER LEARN THAT CASSETTE TAPE IS MADE OF A FORM of the plastic polyethylene, often sold under the trade name Mylar, which is not recyclable. What's worse, the Mylar is coated with toxic metals, especially chromium.

Suddenly I hear a woman's voice. Loud, high-pitched, nearly a scream.

Ami and Achin, the sisters who live in the house and work for my parents, burst into the master bedroom. Arms waving, Ami shrieks, "Smells very bad! Something burning!" The stench from the tapes has reached directly into the kitchen area where they were chopping vegetables. The women had walked the perimeter of the house, terrified there was a dangerous fire, or that one of the cars was in flames, or, given the noxious fumes, that the garden hose had ignited.

Cindy says calmly, "It's okay. We're just getting rid of these."

We are like first responders to our own carnage.

Our mother bursts into the room. My father rushes in next, followed by his attorney. They look at us, their mouths open.

"Jesus Christ!" our father screams. "What the hell are you doing?" He looks over at his attorney. "They're destroying evidence! What if they are called to testify?"

Our father's attorney, Leonard Garment, was former president Nixon's lawyer during Watergate. Len was the one who told Nixon to surrender his tapes to Congress. I can only imagine what he is thinking now. Len looks at the carnage, his shirt sleeves rolled up. He scans the fireplace as he runs his hand through his grey hair, trying to stay calm. "Ladies, I don't think this is the way to go."

Our mother is incapable of words. She is frozen, her mouth a straight line, her emotions under a block of ice, her Swedish ancestry kicking in. Dad, on the other hand, is an opera singer, belting out his fury.

"Who authorized you to do this? What the hell! This is a disaster!"

Len looks over at us. I have no idea what to do. I wish he'd say something more. He must think we're idiots. As Len looks at us, it feels as though I'm being sucked into a vortex or being dropped into a giant blender, that I'm being added to Nixon and Watergate, my father, guys like Haldeman and Erlichman. I'm part of a big scandal smoothie, being blended into crooked history.

18

Being a Wick once opened so many doors for me. I got to experience things most people didn't. Oscar-winning actress Loretta Young was at my wedding, along with actor and singer Rick Nelson and his wife, actress Kris, actor Mark Harmon, not to mention the Reagans. Judy Garland lived next door and the Playboy mansion was down the street. When our father was producing the film for Fox starring the Three Stooges, Moe, Larry, and Curly would stop by our house regularly; Moe once took me for a ride in his powder-blue Thunderbird. Now, the mere mention of our last name spells doom. It seems like ages since we were celebrating Christmas with the Reagans and everything was eggnog-joyful.

I think about my glamorous wedding again. I imagine myself choking on a cheese ball, in my lace wedding gown, guests rushing over, arguing about who does the best Heimlich maneuver, my face bright red from lack of oxygen. Then, as if that weren't bad enough, I pass out on the dance floor of the tented tennis court where our lavish reception was held. My father, in his tux, at the mic, in front of the Les Brown Orchestra, telling everyone the marriage won't last and he might go to prison. The shattered fairy tale is on a loop inside my head.

How did my life reverse itself so drastically? I assumed I would waltz into this next chapter with ease, just as I had done with every other chapter. Instead, it seems I am failing at everything. At my job, I scramble daily to understand almost every detail, acronyms, important names. I am faking it hour by hour and it seems only a matter of time before I am found out. And now, my name—my passport to my job—has become tainted.

I am sitting in my office at my desk at work with the door shut. No one's seen me yet, and I'm dreading the moment when I have to face my colleagues. I know they will look at me differently. How could her father have done that? She only got her job because of her father, and now he's a potential felon.

Then a darker thought occurs to me: I might actually get fired. I'll be a liability. It'll no longer be, "This is Pam Wick, daughter of Charles and Mary Jane, best friends of the president." Now it'll be, "She's no longer with us, she got rehired at Saks Fifth Avenue in Beverly Hills in Better Sportswear."

The knock at my door makes me jump in my seat. Suddenly Nancy Reynolds bounds into my office, full of life, her short blonde hair seeming to shimmer. It is like an explosion of merriness, a kind of assault to my mood.

"Let's go see Barbara Bush," she says enthusiastically.

Barbara Bush? This was the last thing I expected her to say. And I'm not sure how to interpret this. Are we just not going to talk about my father? Or is it possible she doesn't yet know? She reads the papers religiously. That can't possibly be the case.

I am confused and anxious as we glide up Massachusetts Avenue, Nancy behind the wheel of her car. She cheerfully explains that Mrs. Bush has agreed to film a promotional video for the PBS show *Reading Rainbow*. We've been hired by the network to be the liaison with the Second Lady, to make sure everything is coordinated, and that Mrs. Bush is comfortable with the material. I suddenly feel nauseous, looking ahead at the cars on the street. Outside, the sky is grey. I glance over at Nancy, inspecting her face to see if there is a hint that she knows anything. She begins speaking but I don't understand anything she is saying; it's as if I'm wearing thick headphones, her voice is so muffled. I hear the faint sound of the car engine, distant honking. My wool sweater feels itchy on my skin. I am unable to focus.

We pull into the circular driveway of the vice president's house, which is on the grounds of the US Naval Observatory. The Victorian structure with round turrets and broad verandas is so inviting; however, rather than feeling the charm, I feel doom. I don't want to greet Mrs. Bush. I don't want Nancy to say my last name. As we are about to get out of the car, Nancy pauses. I read her face. I brace for the worst.

"I'm sorry about your dad, Pam."

Why is she telling me this now? Is she going to fire me before we see Mrs. Bush? I don't understand. Maybe she didn't want me to make a scene at the office? Nancy's blonde sunniness fades as she continues.

"Listen, this is Washington. Today it's your father, tomorrow, somebody else. You just have to hang in there. He has a good lawyer, I assume?"

I say yes. Nancy nods.

And that's it. I'm not getting fired. At least not now.

I sense, though, she still has questions. She looks at me, and I notice she seems to move slightly away from me, in her seat. Is it my imagination? Or is she actually trying to create some distance between us? For a brief second, I feel like she doesn't want to get any of me on her.

The Garden Room, where we meet, has puffy floral chairs and wicker furniture. The cameraman and his assistant set up while we wait for Mrs. Bush. I try to concentrate on everything Nancy is telling me about the project. But then I also can't stop obsessing about the cameramen near us. I imagine him turning to me and snapping a picture, a quick freelance shot he can sell to the papers.

Moments later, Mrs. Bush walks in, wearing pearls and an enthusiastic smile on her face. I think to myself how gung ho she seems, as though she would jump into a game of tag football, even in pearls. She takes my hand.

"Pam, I just love your ma and pa; so glad to be working with you."

Hasn't she read the papers? Dad recorded *everyone*. Maybe he recorded your husband the vice president, Mrs. Bush?

But she is still smiling, which tells me that either she didn't read the paper, which is unlikely, or that she is being kind to me. Then Mrs. Bush focuses on my face for a moment and I get a different feeling, a sensation that I will start to have a lot over the next months. She looks at me as if she is trying to find something. I can tell she has a question, just as Nancy did, but it's not appropriate for her to ask.

I am relieved when we're finally working, reviewing the promo script. "Pam, how about if I say it *this way*, putting the emphasis on illiteracy?" Mrs. Bush just asked *me*. Why *me*? Nancy is standing right next to me. What did I do, look competent? I don't know what to say. Suddenly I don't even know who I am. I've evaporated; everything I am related to is faltering.

"How about emphasizing the word 'children'?" I suggest, failing to understand how those words popped out of my mouth.

She nods. "I like that; it works."

Mrs. Bush looks into the camera.

"Hi, I'm Barbara Bush. I bet you'd like your children to be excited about reading. Did you know that illiteracy in this country could be eliminated by the year 2000?"

As she speaks, hands folded in her lap, a vase of flowers next to her, it occurs to me that Barbara Bush *is* Washington. She is focused, conducting business at hand. That's how she survives. That's how Washington survives. Things get done. The turbulence of scandals notwithstanding.

19

I return to my parents' house after work, feeling drained. As I step into the kitchen I see my father angrily waving a *Time* magazine. I forget about my day and I'm now more concerned about seeing my dad.

"I agree, Charles. It's not good," my mother says from the kitchen, where she's making dinner.

"Not good? It's preposterous!" he yells.

As I watch my father standing there, red-faced, furious, I am bulldozed by his display of anger. I've seen it before, but this is turbo-charged, and it worries me because beneath the anger, I smell fear. Fear is not something I've ever seen in my father. Yet, somehow, I recognize the slight hint of it—the way he pauses before belting out angry words, the way his eyes keep moving, as if searching for something, maybe safety.

It turns out my father is featured in this week's *Time* magazine—it's the January 9th issue of 1984 and the new year has barely begun; his lawyer Len got him an advance copy. It's not a flattering story. I ask to read it. *How bad can it be*, I think as I carry the magazine into the living room. On the cover is a picture of Pope John Paul II appearing to forgive the man who planned to assassinate him. I wonder if my father will be forgiven.

The article about Dad is titled, "A Reagan Crony On The Line." I roll the word "crony" around in my mind. It sounds like Dad is merely a buddy of the president, that my father got his job just because they're friends. I know my father is well qualified to run the USIA. I list his accomplishments in my mind: lawyer; he built a healthcare company comprising a chain of nursing homes and took it public; as a professional musician he arranged music for Tommy Dorsey and traveled with the orchestra; and he was a William Morris literary agent.

Then I read the opening sentence of the article, "Flamboyant Charles Wick admits to making secret tapes...." Flamboyant? How can they call my father "flamboyant?" He's not a flashy guy. Most of his suits are grey or navy. He does have one pair of velvet Christmas pants with a tiny holly berry pattern that my mother picked out. But flamboyant?

"He travels surrounded by four bodyguards," the article continues.

Dad flies all over the world for his job. He will eventually go to all or most of those countries on that big map in his office. It is dangerous in places. I also know that my father has had threats against his life from the Soviets. When my mother learned this, she snuck a cigarette and stood by the window in my bedroom, fanning the smoke outside, telling me not to tell anyone about her smoking or the threats against my father.

And then I read, "he stays in $200-a-night hotel suites." If this was coming out of the taxpayer's pocket, I would understand the outrage. But my parents pay for these rooms out of their budget, not the government's.

"...and he hands out $5 tips." Why didn't they ask before they printed this? I could have told them that he tips bigger than five dollars. More like ten or twenty dollars. Growing up we got used to our father stopping on the way out of a restaurant and handing the busboy cash. "This guy's working hard; you kids are lucky, never forget that." Dad understands what it's like to work hard at a menial job for very little.

When he was a kid, he toiled after school at his father's scrap metal business. He has held on to that memory.

These people at *Time* magazine do not understand my father. They are seeing somebody else, and I want to tell them that they need to come over and sit down and get to know him. I want to usher this *Time* journalist in and take out our scrapbooks and family photos, especially of my grandparents in Cleveland, and explain how decent my father is. "Do you understand that he did this all himself? He actually believes he is making a difference in this world."

The only part of the article that is not critical of my father is when it mentions that "the USIA was a 'neglected foreign policy backwater' before Charles Wick became its director." Under my father, the rusty, aging equipment of Voice of America has been updated. Several months earlier, when the Soviets shot down a Korean Airlines passenger plane with 269 people on board, my father got his hands on the dramatic audio tape of the Soviet pilot discussing with ground-control officers whether to shoot down the plane. He created a riveting presentation shown at the UN Security Council—and to the world. The Soviets finally admitted culpability, although not fully. My father is deeply proud of that moment and his contribution to a crucial international event.

I put the magazine down and stare out the French doors to the icy garden. It feels like a tsunami of bad is crashing onto us. This article, the photographers, the congressional investigation. I want to hide in bed. I want to go back to California. The walls of this house feel porous, as though all these bad things are seeping in and settling on the furniture, on the floor, and all over us, like toxic dust. Seeing my parents upset, it's as though they are covered in a bad microscopic powder that they can't brush off, no matter how hard they try.

And now *Time* magazine is spreading more bad dust. *Everyone* flips through *Time* magazine. It's a household name with its crisp red border. And now, my father is immortalized as a "flamboyant" "crony" in this respected weekly with the pope on the cover, and people everywhere—my friends, my parents' friends, my father's business associates, my fifth-grade teacher—will read it and, even if they don't believe all of what is written, they will still wonder.

Then I start to wonder myself. Do I see my father as he is or is there a slightly different version? Am I so biased that I have no idea that he might have character traits that are questionable? I scan the article, once again. "Within the USIA, Wick is regarded as temperamental and high-handed by much of his staff...some complain that Wick's idea for the Voice of America to broadcast editorials undermines the station's credibility, though regular news broadcasts continue to be unbiased."

I am left with a burdensome, nagging thought that will stay with me over the coming weeks: Is it possible that *Time* magazine is right?

20

I ask Pam what she thought of the *Time* article. I want an unbiased opinion and she's the ideal person: She understands Washington and seems to care about me.

She stares out my office window, and when she finally speaks, it's as if she's choosing her words carefully.

"People are complicated. Most are a mix of ambition and flaws. When held to the light, there are little fractures in all of us...."

There is silence. I'm not sure if she's thinking about what to say next, or if that is the end of her answer.

Is she saying my father is fractured? I think back on his rise to success—I've heard the story since I was little. His immigrant parents, their Russian accents, their small house in Cleveland where he and his sister grew up. His father worked in scrap-metal yards.

For me, he's an example of someone who has done life right, who made it on his own with no advantages; he fought his way to the top. Is Pam questioning my father? Does she see a different version of him? Does she see something in him I don't see? I thought she'd reassure me. I want her to say more, to move this big thought off of me. But she doesn't. She just looks at me, her serious eyes seeming to search me with questions. I've never seen her silent before.

21

As kids, my dad taught us the importance of being honest. Abraham Lincoln and Benjamin Franklin were among his examples. "Honesty is the best policy," he would tell us over and over. I would know he was serious because his voice would become very low, and he would look each of us in the eye. I never lied. But once, Kim did. When she was about six, she scribbled in red pen on our coveted World Book Encyclopedias. The glossy books, off-white with faux-gold-leaf letters, were marred with red Pentel ink. My mother was the one who found them. At first Kim lied: "I didn't do that." Then she confessed. She had to stay in her room all evening. No TV for a month. She had broken a golden rule, the one that said we should never lie.

We had to speak up if we saw something wrong, we had to be kind to strangers, and we had to basically do unto others what we would have them do unto us, even when we felt disinclined. Life was defined for us and there were rules to be followed—rules that ensured we were good citizens within our family and in our community.

Once, my brothers threw all the neighbor's pool furniture into her pool. When our father found out, he called the police and had an officer in black-and-white uniform come to the house and sit down to reprimand my brothers. Then they had to apologize to the neighbor.

My father grounded them for a month—no friends, no TV. They never went near the neighbor's pool again.

Another time, my parents drove to UCLA to pick up my best friend and me from the annual fair. We were supposed to meet near the entrance, and when we didn't show up, my father alerted security; my parents were terrified. We finally showed up two hours later and, after we dropped off my friend, my parents questioned me again about why we were late. I told them that it was my friend's idea to keep playing the coin toss to win prizes, even though we were running late. My father responded sarcastically that since my best friend was such a bad influence on me, I was not to see her for two months—no sleepovers, no after-school dates, no weekend get-togethers. That's what I got for blaming my friend. The punishment was tailor-made for me.

The result was the creation of a life that seemed like a jigsaw puzzle of perfection. There were tough consequences when a piece would go missing.

I never questioned my father's advice because he was so perfect, too. Today, like every other day, he sits up straight with perfect posture, his custom suit freshly pressed, his wavy hair smoothed with pomade. My mother too appears cover ready for *W* magazine—her Adolfo suit, chunky gold earrings, and polished nails. The three of us are in The Jockey Club, where, in fact, everyone *is* perfect. Women in Chanel suits, jackets with large shoulders, pussybow blouses, and men in expensive looking suits and ties. It's a parade of perfection. Senators, ambassadors, journalists, and dignitaries dine on crab cakes, lamb chops, and freshly caught fish. Jackie Kennedy used to be a regular and Mrs. R eats here often. George Will is at a table near the entrance and my parents and I are in a booth.

I notice how self-assured my father seems in our booth, as if there is no scandal happening. He is perfect. Don't question him. This is all going to be fine. It's all good.

Then he stifles a yawn, rubs his eyes, and completely lets down his guard. He looks exhausted. He says that he'd rather be at home. "We have to be in public, put on a good face, per Len. Last thing I wanted to do, frankly."

And with that, I know he is not doing well. He's beleaguered, putting up a front. He is desperately trying to appear like everything is okay. After all, that is what we do in my family.

When I was six years old, I was in the middle of a stylish party being thrown by my parents to honor the composer Meredith Willson and his wife Rini, a Russian opera singer. I was in the living room with my siblings, in my best robe and slippers, greeting guests. This was a tradition, meeting guests. If we were "good" we were awarded a Shirley Temple drink before we went back up to our rooms.

"How are you?" A beautifully dressed woman looked down at six-year-old me.

I hesitated, then answered, "I don't know."

My father, dapper in suit and tie, quickly took my hand, led me to the other side of the living room. "Darling, that is not an answer."

Then he took me to my room and in a firm and punitive voice told me, "You stay here until you figure out how to answer correctly."

I couldn't understand his change in tone from calling me "darling" just moments ago and then reprimanding me harshly. I was being punished.

"'Fine, thank you,' is the proper answer," he said as he walked out of my room. I repeated the words silently to myself. "I'm fine, thank you." That was the answer for perfect little girls. Then I said it to myself a few more times, to make sure I had it down correctly.

I had not been perfect at my parents' cocktail party. I did not represent a well-raised child that my parents had worked so hard to create. I strayed from the narrative.

Now at The Jockey Club, my mother, father, and I are putting on a good face. By being in this important restaurant, by knowing the maître d', by sitting in booth number two—the power booth—we are fine, thank you. Only we know we are dangling by a thread.

I notice dark circles under my father's eyes. He hasn't been sleeping.

"Len has been by my side throughout this whole goddamned thing." There is even a harsh edge to his voice that wasn't there before.

As he tells us the story of his day with Len in New York, I notice a drop in the octave of his typically cheerful tone, and I suspect that something bad is coming. Dad tells us that at lunch Len urged him to go to a phone booth in the lobby of the hotel where the restaurant was located and call former President Jimmy Carter. Len wanted my father to apologize for taping Carter on a phone call months ago, when he called to congratulate him on the nuclear nonproliferation treaty.

"I don't know how to tell you this," my father says as he turns to us. "I can't quite believe it myself. Jesus, it's unbelievable."

I have no idea what he's about to say and I am worried. He proceeds to declare to me and my mother that he went to the phone booth and dialed the number Len gave him. The former president personally answered his phone. My father then apologized to Carter who listened, then was silent for several moments.

"Jimmy Carter asked me to get down on my knees *in the phone booth* and to pray telephonically with him!"

As my father says this, it's as if he still can't believe it himself.

"Did you actually get down on your knees?"

Dad turns to me and simply says "yes" as if it was obviously the right thing to do.

I think about it: My father on his knees? In a phone booth? The image of him—chin level with the coin return, whispering scripture into the pay phone to a former US president—turns my world upside down. I can't believe I'm hearing this. On his knees? My father, the lawyer, Hollywood producer, William Morris agent, Tommy Dorsey big-band arranger, blockbuster businessman. I look over at him, I try to reconcile the big-time him with the fractured him. I can't.

I think of my grandparents and their modest house, where we'd sit on the porch and eat my grandmother's chopped liver and stuffed cabbage. Inside, their furniture would be covered in plastic slipcovers. Once, at a cocktail reception at the British Embassy, my father referred to his father as a businessman and venture capitalist. I didn't say anything. I knew why he did that and it made me sad. I just smiled and quietly sipped my drink.

I look at Dad and realize how ashamed he must feel. Not only about taping telephone calls, but shame is such a large piece of who he really is. His shame of being a poor kid with immigrant parents never went away; it just got covered up by the grandeur of his life. I never understood that until now. I have no idea how to dig him out, pick him up.

22

As if my father's shame couldn't get any worse, he now looks defeated as he sits at the witness table at a congressional hearing. He faces a congressman seated on an elevated dais, an imposing wooden structure, flanked by an American flag, with a carved eagle at its center.

My father is in a tailored, dark suit with his best shirt and cufflinks, his hair perfectly in place. I know my mother used a tiny bit of her hairspray to pat down potential strays. This was her entire contribution to the proceedings. I am here in place of my mother, to spare her the pain and humiliation. Today a bill is on the table to make taping telephone conversations without notifying the other party a federal crime, and my father is the star witness.

"For the record...we are not here to impeach Charlie Wick or to cause him any additional pain, but certainly he and his associates have done a good job of that already." The opening words of the hearing are spoken by Texas Democratic Congressman Jack Brooks. I'm still nervous about the hearing, but I like the way the congressman calls my dad "Charlie."

There is endless back-and-forth on the technicalities of the existing law, but I don't register most of it. I am worried about my father, but the technical terms lull me into a false sense that nothing important will be resolved today. The words fly through the air as I listen. Phrases like "consent of all parties," "determinations," "policies," "records administration," "GSA regulations," "elevated statutory law," "policy guidance," "privacy act 1974" surround me.

However, California Democratic Congressman Henry Waxman gets my attention. Waxman is aggressive; he's out to get my dad, I can tell. He doesn't call my father Charlie like Congressman Brooks. He doesn't call him anything. Waxman stares menacingly down at Dad, grilling him about his taping telephone conversations, particularly in Florida and California where taping is a criminal act.

"Did you tape President Reagan?"

"No, sir."

Waxman continues.

"But you taped former President Carter. So, you tape former presidents but not current presidents?"

Dad skillfully evades the question and talks about details of the telephone call instead.

Waxman doesn't let up. He looks around the hearing room.

"I suspect he's gone further than taping surreptitiously."

Then, suddenly, it feels as if Waxman's attention is aimed at *me*.

"I want to know if you, or anyone that works for you, or anyone acting under your direction, has destroyed any of these tapes?"

The words pour over me like molten lava. Did Dad know he was going to ask him *this*? I look at the back of my father's head, wondering what his face is telling the room.

"No, sir," my father responds softly.

"So, you have those tapes?" Waxman glares at him.

I shrink in my chair, pulling my arm onto my lap, as if a dangling limb will incriminate me. The room is quiet. Then Dad answers again.

"Oh, no. I haven't destroyed any tapes."

Henry Waxman is like a bulldog ripping at Dad's leg.

"Do you have them? Are they in your possession?"

"No, I have destroyed no personal tapes."

This goes on for what seems like hours. A terrifying scenario begins to play out in my head. I imagine my father blurting out to the hearing room, "My daughters destroyed the tapes, not me!" He has been pushed to the edge and reduced to a puddle of nervous confession. I am just waiting for a bailiff to walk over to me and place handcuffs on my wrists, the beginning of twenty years in prison for destruction of evidence. I imagine my father watching helplessly, the hearing room silent. I will never get another job. No one will hire me with a prison record. I am front page *New York Times*, a nasty piece by William Safire. "Apple Doesn't Fall Far...Wick's Daughter Indicted."

The hearing finally ends, and, miraculously, I am still a free woman. My father has given his testimony and the bill will be voted on when it is finalized by the committee.

* * *

IN THE CAR I ASK MY FATHER IF HE KNEW whether he would be questioned over the destruction of tapes. He didn't expect it, he tells me, adding that it threw him a bit at first. Still, Dad knew that the tapes had been destroyed and it could perhaps be considered that he was withholding evidence.

"What would you do if they found out? Would you tell about us burning the tapes?"

He glances over at me and manages a bemused smile.

"Frankly, you wouldn't do well in prison."

23

It is heartbreaking to see my father sit alone at the dining room table. His shoulders slumped, he stares down at unopened files. Since dinner last night nothing has changed. It makes me so sad. I want to help him, but I don't know how. His camel-colored cashmere sweater and crisp shirt remind me that he is one of "the Top People." He can afford the best. But now the sweater seems saggy, too large. As if he's so diminished it no longer fits.

And then I get angry, which surprises me. I am angry for him not being who he said he is. He is supposed to be strong. I am surprised and baffled. He's uncertain; he's not him. And it scares me. He created our world, made up all the rules. "I'm just telling you how it's done in the big time. You do this, *this* way, and your life will be X. Be right. Be like us." Why did he tell me how to be when he didn't know himself?

My foundation no longer feels solid. Everything is wobbly. I don't recognize my life; I start to question everything. What does it all mean? How do I know anything? How do I rely on anything? What is success? What does it mean to be a good person?

I think of the Wizard of Oz. My father is the little man behind the curtain, desperately trying to work the dials: "Don't look behind the curtain." But I have, and it has blown my world open.

24

On Sunday morning, there is no one to eat breakfast with. The house is quiet, except for the voices of my parents with their lawyer in the living room.

"Goddammit, Len, I'm doing everything I can."

"Charles, he's just trying to help us."

My parents sound urgent and desperate. Dad's scandal is the beast that must be fed—voraciously gobbling up long strategy sessions, worry, fear, my father's apologies, extra shots of vodka, and my mother's anxiety, which she channels into daily phone calls with Mrs. R. The scandal beast is demanding, threatening, and hungry. It is insatiable.

I step down the hallway; light slices through the floor-to-ceiling windows. Cody the Doberman trots up to me. I pet his muzzle. We continue toward the kitchen, our gaits synchronized. We are not feeding the beast; we're on the sidelines, helpless. The kitchen is quiet, too. I fill a glass with water, listening to the sound of my own breathing. Dishes drying on the rack, an empty coffee pot, stacks of newspapers with enemy ink. I am part of a still life. Just standing in the kitchen, unmoving, alone. I don't want to be in this moment. Suddenly, I feel the need to escape the house and the cloud of doom hanging over it, even if it's only for a while.

I call Pam Curtis hoping she'll meet me for breakfast. *Please, answer your phone!* Her phone rings several times, and when she doesn't answer I call my sister Cindy in New York. I tell her how I'm feeling.

"Why don't you go out by yourself? Everyone does it."

I imagine myself sitting in a restaurant, alone. How lonely. But I have to try. There is a little part inside of me that pushes me forward, that wants to get out, away from the constant battle inside our house. Plus, Cindy tells me that when she moved to Manhattan, she went out by herself all the time.

"You just bring a book. It's fun."

My parents' bookshelf is filled, so I find a page-turner my mother recommended and slip it into my tote.

A nearby coffee shop looks inviting—colonial brick and flower window boxes. As I enter, it smells like Mom's pancakes and bacon, which is comforting. For a moment I'm back in Los Angeles, in the safety of our family kitchen, no scandal, no press camped outside our house. I try to keep this good feeling in my mind as I stand in line, surrounded by families with kids.

"Just one?" the hostess motions to me. The good feeling vanishes. *Please, not so loud*, I want to tell her. I don't want to be noticed as the only single in the restaurant. Why doesn't anyone say "just two" or "just a family" or "just a couple"?

The hostess leads me to a table in the middle of the restaurant.

"Is there something maybe more private?" I ask, feeling self-conscious.

She just drops the menu on the table, motioning to a family behind me to take an empty booth. Reluctantly, I put down my tote and settle into my seat. I am so mad at myself for feeling overwhelmed. It's just breakfast, for God's sake.

"Pam, is that you?"

It is a colleague from work. He and his family stare at me from a booth. They look so perfect and happy together. I feel like an accident they've slowed down to watch. *You're alone because you're reading a book—it's fine*, I tell myself. I wish they'd stop looking at me. But they don't. Now I can imagine they feel sorry for me because of my father, the press, the nightly news. I must be carrying the residue of scandal, too. How can I not? They must see me under the same cloud of doom as my parents. I thought I could escape by leaving the house, but I can't. So, after a moment, I say "Hi!" then walk over. Will, my colleague, introduces me to his wife and kids, who politely greet me. Now the restaurant begins to spin, voices start stretching like taffy, my heart thumps inside my chest. I try to cover all of this by grinning widely.

"Hey, hang in there," Will says, with a knowing look. He's referring to my father's scandal, no doubt. His wife nods.

"Nice to meet you." As I walk back to my table, I *know* they feel sorry for me. I would if I were them. They must also feel sorry for me for being alone.

I am truly alone, I realize. My father, through no fault of his own, for the first time in his life, is unable to be there for me. And I feel a kind of solitude. It's as though my father has become a phantom limb. His devotion to me and his interest in the mundane details of my life have morphed into just the sensation of him, the feeling of him. He doesn't do the things he once did. He no longer looks at me with all his attention when I ask a question, pausing, considering. He hurriedly tosses out a stock answer off the shelf, while his phantom self still considers what to say.

25

What I hate most days about work is that instant when I step off the elevator. Typically, a group of my coworkers stand around chatting in front of the polished-wood bureau stacked with the *Washington Post*, the *Washington Times*, the *New York Times* (it's a game of Russian roulette to see whether my father will be in print). They always look up when they see me. I get sympathetic smiles, insincere hellos, extra-long stares. But underneath all of this, I feel there is curiosity, judgment, and dislike, even. It feels so awkward. I want to disappear. *How could he have done that*, they must be thinking. I anticipate this, setting off for the office each morning. By the time I arrive I have worked myself up to a near panic attack.

Today at work, it's my task to get a list of the upcoming House and Senate committee hearings. It's a simple enough request; I should know how to do this. My mind swirls. Committees...Energy and Commerce, Environment and Public Works...I read and studied this, I know these committees, but at the moment I am blanking. My mind is a scramble. I can't think.

I bolt down the hallway to Pam's office. I can ask Pam a million questions—she doesn't fault me for not knowing the answers. "The dumb ones are those who don't ask questions," she always tells me. When I'm about to cut myself off from talking too long—a constant habit—because I think I might sound ignorant, Pam urges me to continue, "Go on, you have the floor, Pam Wick." This is often accompanied by a laugh; not a laugh *at* me, but a laugh *in honor of me,* as if she is saying my insecurity is so laughable, it shouldn't even be allowed in the room. It touches me, her kindness. I can relax around Pam; I don't have to be on guard.

"Pam, what you know is valuable in the world," she reminds me constantly.

One time we were at the National Gallery for a Monet exhibition. I was so excited to show Pam the paintings. We were standing before the cool blues and violets of the *Water Lilies.* I noticed Pam squinting, focusing on the vast canvases. Then she turned to me.

"Explain. I never studied art."

So, I told her about Monet's obsession with light and color, and how his tiny brushstrokes of juxtaposing different colors appear as one color if you step back and look at his paintings. Pam glanced back at the canvas. I noticed a satisfied look on her face, and I was happy that I had filled gaps in her knowledge, that I had satisfied a curiosity, and that she seemed content—all because of me. As if what I had to say were really important. I loved that moment because I felt so comfortable, like I belonged.

Now as I stand in Pam's office, I realize it is empty. I stand there for a minute not knowing what to do. I am thrust back into the same sense of solitude I felt at the restaurant the day before, the feeling that I have to fend for myself. But of course, I *can* fend for myself. All at once, it hits that I have *me.* This is the first time this thought has occurred to me. The small part of myself that pushed me forward to go out for breakfast, the one that has a little courage, tells me that it's okay, I am not alone. Is this part of me now? Or was it always there?

I can do this. The Library of Congress, that's where I can get a list of the upcoming Senate and House committee hearings. I grab my coat and tote and rush back down the hallway toward the elevator.

I find the librarian who points me in the direction of the area where I can locate the schedule of Congressional hearings. Ten minutes later I have the pages in my hands. As I wait in line in to make a photocopy, I gaze around the Main Reading Room of the Thomas Jefferson Building, struck by the beauty of this space. There is an enormous, golden dome ceiling glistening in afternoon light. I stare up at the giant marble columns, the female figures in plaster atop each, and male bronze statues on the balustrades. I read the plaque carved in marble at the entrance, a description of the painting on the dome above me:

> *On the ceiling of the lantern, which rises above the highest part of the dome, is a painting of a beautiful female figure representing Human Understanding.... She is attended by two cherubs: one is holding the book of wisdom and knowledge and the other seems, by his gesture, to be encouraging viewers beneath to persist in their struggle toward perfection.*

I reread the last line. Struggle toward perfection?

I glance around and see people sitting at desks and standing at the reference area, carrying books, whispering to each other. Is that what they're doing, trying to be perfect? In Washington, it seems like perfection is often the only goal worth attaining. Even the buildings have to be perfect. But are they really? Underneath the polished marble of the monuments, the Capitol building, the congressional office buildings, there are beams, joints, nails, reinforced cement.

I feel an urge to warn everyone. It's all a ruse. What they told you isn't true. There is only a façade covering grit and metal, dirt.

26

If the buildings in Washington seem perfect, and they really aren't underneath, I realize that I too am similarly imperfect underneath. My pleasing smile, my effort to always be nice to people—"yes, of course," "how lovely,"—so much of my life has been spent keeping up a smooth, polished finish. And underneath all of this is the real me, the gritty me, the me that gets angry, sad, scared, the me that holds up the perfect me for all the world to see. But these past months have shown me that being perfect is nearly impossible. This is Washington, and I am tired of holding out the perfect me.

Part of being smooth and perfect is that I have always been afraid to be seen as a fighter. It would seem too aggressive. I have tried my whole life to be the peacemaker, to not make waves. As a kid, I would say "yes" often when I meant "no." I would never show my anger. In school, even when other kids were mean, I'd pretend they weren't. I'd be nice to them, though underneath I would be upset.

But today is different. Today, we are fighting back.

I flip through the pages of the *New York Times* looking for my sister Cindy's small but significant counterattack. She's an artist with a mission today. Cindy creates political drawings for the editorial page, and she's given me a heads-up about her subtle but clever "takedown" of the very newspaper that tarnished our father's image.

Her Cold War-era cartoon features two men—a US special negotiator and the Soviet Ambassador—walking in the woods, trying to reach an agreement on arms control. But that's not the point. "Look in the leaves," Cindy had told me. A tree, in the foreground, branches thick with foliage, covers up a message Cindy has written. "Fuck Safire" is visible there if you know where to look.

Hooray for my sister. And all of us! It's as if I just popped a button on the straitjacket of appeasement I've worn my whole life.

I race down the hallway and bound into Pam's office to show her.

Pam howls with laughter, "You have to show Anne!"

Anne Wexler, a cofounder of the firm, stops by for her meeting with Pam and leans over the newspaper, scrutinizing Cindy's handiwork. She suddenly lets out a gut-belly laugh. A firestorm of comic relief explodes from her. In all her years of Washington scandals, congressional investigations, and even Watergate, she has yet to see *this*, she tells us. The sound of Anne's laughter is like a signal to me that she's on my side. The more we laugh, the more at home I feel.

It feels so good to fight back, instead of taking things lying down. My whole body begins to relax, and I feel a sense of expansiveness, as if it might be okay for me to take up more space in the room, in my own life.

27

"I need you. Just take notes, back me up."

Anne is at the door to my office, asking me to help her. For once, this doesn't terrify me the way it used to. Lately, I have a new sense of confidence—the idea that I might possibly be qualified for my job. Besides my tiny Library of Congress victory, there have been others. The New York Power Authority guys, on their last trip here, said they appreciated my memo on the benefits of Canadian hydropower. I found material in the library which helped me understand and create a cohesive document. Barbara Bush even took my suggestion for the *Reading Rainbow* promo.

Now, Anne needs *me*. Back *her* up? I can stand behind her and have a ready answer. If she stumbles (which I can't imagine), I'm there to catch her. As if I'm her Michael Deaver, President Reagan's chief of staff. I know that's a big stretch, ridiculous, actually, but I'm feeling optimistic. It is the first time since I moved to DC.

However, my confidence wanes a little bit when I look at a briefing memo for today's meeting.

SUBJECT: Railroad - Coal Slurry Legislation

Coal slurry? What *is* coal slurry?

Slurry...sounds like Slurpee? A Slurpee with coal?

I read through the file. Slurry, I learn, is a mixture of water and pulverized coal. The slurry moves through a pipeline to the power plant. Then it is dried and burned as fuel. So, it *is* like a Slurpee—a slushy substance sucked through a giant pipeline. I imagine a giant straw lying from Wyoming to Texas, a loud slurping sound as the coal slurry is sucked through to the power plant.

I read on. Coal is then transported by freight train. But transporting coal by rail is expensive and consumers pay with high electric bills. A coal slurry pipeline would reduce costs significantly. However, it would also deprive our clients, the railroad industry, of its primary revenue source. The Coal Pipeline Act of 1983 was defeated in Congress last year. Our client, the American Association of Railroads, was jubilant about the defeat of the bill. So, our firm, I have to assume, succeeded for its client.

Now, the railroad guys are meeting to strategize in the event of any future proposed legislation.

Half an hour later, I am seated around the conference table with fifteen railroad executives. Most are beefy-looking guys in tight shirts, stretchy polyester blazers, slicked back hair, and one is wearing cowboy boots. Anne is at the head of the table, and I sit to her left. Coffee and plates of pastries are in the middle of the table.

I start to take notes. Slurry, pipeline, trains, electricity. My hand is writing so fast trying to get the important information down.

About ten minutes later I look up and notice the guy across from me, waving his arms animatedly, almost yelling.

"I told the goddamned congressman, just because he thinks coal is dirty doesn't mean we gotta roll over and take it up the—pardon the expression, ladies—wazoo."

I notice that Anne appears unflappable.

"Roger, listen to me. Your job as head of CSX rail is to make that congressman willing to talk to you. You do not get in a—pardon the expression, gentlemen—a goddamned pissing contest."

No one says anything. Roger chews quietly on a pastry scrap. It's as if Anne's lassoed these guys like cattle, only they seem to be loutish cowboys.

I continue taking notes and, as I do, I try to concentrate, but I keep imagining these guys coming home to their wives, loosening their tight collars, and telling them about "that Anne Wexler." She is powerful, she is purposeful, she is perfect. I realize that I still have so much left to learn, that Anne has just created a new standard for me to live up to.

As we head out of the conference room after the group of men, Anne looks down at her feet and spots something. We both stop abruptly.

"Oh my God, I can't believe it," she starts to laugh.

I too look down at Anne's feet. Her shoes are mismatched. She is wearing one brown pump and one navy one. Serious shoes.

Anne's laugh explodes. A deep, delightful sound. She grabs my arm to steady herself, balancing files in her other hand. She's laughing so hard. A few of the guys look back at her. Anne waves them forward out of the room. She turns to me.

"Always make sure you turn the lights on when you get dressed at six a.m.!"

I have witnessed Anne's humanness, that little chink in her armor, and a crack opens up inside of me, a tiny sliver of freedom. Anne is not perfect and she can laugh about it. Everyone is a bit tattered around the edges, no matter how hard they try to pretend they're not. So, maybe, I can be, too?

28

Riding home after work on the subway, I smell the scent of dampened newspapers and notice wet umbrellas from the rain outside. I watch people ending their workday, some reading, others just sitting quietly. I hear the whoosh of the metro gliding through town. It dawns on me that I am part of all of this. I am a business commuter. For so long I have felt like an outsider, as if I wasn't supposed to be here. But now I am one of many. There is something comforting about this. It's a little awakening and I am grateful.

Moments later, walking up Connecticut Avenue toward my parents' home, the sidewalk is drenched from the rain. A few yards ahead, I spot a "For Rent" sign—a square affixed to a metal pole in the grass, in front of a small brick building. And it hits me. What would it be like to get my own place? What is stopping me? I have my own income, my own job. It's even starting to feel like I have my own life.

As I think about this, my excitement spreads until I am electrified by its presence. Will I paint my walls cobalt blue? What if I fill my refrigerator with only Ben & Jerry's? What if I hang a big window box out my balcony and fill it with orange geraniums? I love them. I've never had a place to put them before. I could tack to a wall my Sierra Club poster with the image of Big Sur, the fog wrapping around the cliffs. I wouldn't have to shove wedding photos into silver picture frames and polish them every weekend. I could do whatever I wanted; it'd be all mine.

The idea of moving out fills me with joy and adrenaline, but more than anything, it floods me with a sense of relief. Life with my parents isn't what it used to be. Dinners with my parents used to be fun, full of music and laughter, everyone talking at once about the latest phone call with one of my siblings, me describing my latest work adventure, my father telling us of the newest USIA satellite news program, the Voice of America's latest penetration behind the iron curtain. And the jokes: My father lobbing a new one. Bursts of laughter, and more jokes. And my parents' optimism that the world was going to be okay—Lebanon would find peace, Soviet disinformation would end, and the federal deficit would be reduced. And the firmly held conviction that we were all making a difference by coming to Washington.

However, my father is falling apart, and I don't recognize my family anymore. And now there is no laughter, no music; the jokes are flat, or nonexistent. Just scotch and silence and the latest legal advice from my father's attorney Len.

"Senator so-and-so needs to hear from you."

"There was another piece in the *Times*. We're offering a rebuttal."

I feel like I am floating in liquid, watching my parents, and I am unable to reach them. I realize that they too are in liquid, and they are floating slowly away from me. In fact, they don't even see me.

It is through no fault of theirs. They are simply surviving. How can I blame them? Even thinking this I feel a little sad, as if I'm abandoning them. How can I even consider moving out? They need me right now. I need to be there for them. I feel a slight anticipatory homesickness and walk a little faster up the street toward their house. How can I just leave?

29

"Mom, I saw this 'For Rent' sign."

I say this from where I'm sitting near my mother in the hair salon, the next day. Her hairdresser, Armand, a wiry man in a brightly-colored silk shirt, is animatedly talking while back-combing her hair.

My mother doesn't even hear me. Armand laughs loudly at something my mother said, as he leans over her. They are like two best friends, gossiping, pretending they're solving world problems. My heart sinks.

Armand continues.

"Can you imagine? Dress was short and patent pumps?"

Why won't he shut up? He is one long, run-on sentence. He's egging her on. This has been going on for nearly a half hour.

I look around the salon. The well-heeled women are pampered, shampooed, gossiping, sipping coffee, receiving manicures and pedicures. This is *the* salon in the Watergate apartment complex, a who's who of women, many with the Reagan administration through their husbands. The whine of blow-dryers, the peripatetic bursts of laughter, and the occasional serious notes. All enwrapped by smells of perfume and sweet shampoo.

My palms are sweaty; I want to say something to my mother. Finally, I get up the nerve to mention the apartment. But then I hesitate. I think about how being at the salon must be a huge escape for my mother. Maybe the only place she feels safe and remotely happy these days. So now I'm going to put a damper on this, to suggest I move out? I can't do it to her.

"Honey, did you say something?"

"No. Nothing."

"Mrs. Wick, good, no brassy color, see?"

Armand holds a mirror out so she can inspect the back of her hair.

But then I can't help myself. I know she will be happy for me.

"Mom, I saw a 'For Rent' sign. I'm going to get an apartment."

I just blurt it out as if I didn't have any control over my actions, my words moving faster than my thoughts.

Her eyebrows rise slightly. I notice a slight smile come to her lips. Relieved, I proceed to tell her about the sign and how I can't stop thinking about it.

To my surprise, she is overly enthusiastic. "This is good news!"

The thing about my mother is that she cares. Even though I'm aware that my parents control and manage my life, and it drives me crazy, I know they think they're doing their best to protect me. Right now, my mother is just happy, excited for me, and, I can tell, will do everything in her power to help me.

"Honey. Where?"

Armand jumps into the conversation, as though I were talking to him.

"Your own place? Yes, good for you," he says.

He continues as if I asked him for his opinion.

"I remember my first place, tiny shoe box. Q Street. Wall-to-wall carpet. Aah, life..."

I have hijacked the gossip and now it's as if my mother and her hairdresser are a cheerleading squad for my life. Mom is elated. I can tell the wheels are clicking in her head as she pops a piece of spearmint candy into her mouth.

"Let's see. You need light, closet space, a little dining area. That's important."

Instead of upsetting her by mentioning my desire to move out, I have given her a new project. She is dreaming up ideas for décor, for how to throw my first dinner party, and how I can finally use that silver gravy boat from my wedding gifts. I don't bother to tell her I have no intention of making gravy.

I wonder how I misapprehended the idea of my moving out this much. I thought I was holding it all together for my parents, that they needed to lean on me, even though I'm not exactly lean-able. But I realize that making sure *I* am okay is more important to them. Their wellbeing (though iffy at the moment) is so intertwined with my own. I feel such a release, such overwhelming relief, like I just moved a giant boulder out of my path. I take a big breath from my toes up.

Armand sprays my mother's hair, shellacking the blonde bouffant French twist with hairspray. The shape is now frozen into a solid piece that will last her until her next appointment next week. Like all her friends, her hair is now the signature Republican coif. My siblings and I often refer lovingly to my mother and her friends as "helmet heads."

"Pam," Armand says as he turns to me. I notice some leftover lunch in his front teeth.

"I fix your mother's hair so good, she could fall out of helicopter and not a hair will be out of place." This is followed by a snort-filled laugh.

My parents are going to Camp David this weekend, and Armand made an extra special effort to give my mother's hair the royal treatment.

An hour later we're leaving the hair salon. My mother with her perfect hair, and me with the relief that I can start searching for apartments.

"Let's take a look. That 'For Rent' sign."

"The apartment?" I'm surprised.

"Sure, why not?" My mother says as we get into her car.

"I didn't take down a number from the sign."

"We'll go ask the manager," she says confidently.

I'm not sure about this but my mother is. We arrive where I had seen the sign and park our car, stepping up to the front of the three-story art deco building. The scent of apple and pear blossom trees fills the air.

"Wonderful old building," Mom says, picking off some dead leaves under pansies in a big pot by the entrance. As we enter and reach the front desk I explain to the older uniformed attendant with bushy brows that I'd like to take a look at the available apartment.

"The garden one-bedroom? Here, call this number." He hands me a card.

My mother looks at him, smiling elegantly.

"Just a peek while we're here?" She is so beautiful, her blonde hair freshly shellacked into her customary French twist, a touch of gold jewelry. How can he refuse her?

"I'm not authorized, ma'am. Sorry."

But this, I know, won't stop her. The expression on Mom's face tells me that she is figuring out a way to see my potential new apartment no matter what. As the attendant turns away from us to answer the intercom, my mother scopes out some glass doors nearby. I realize what she's doing. The glass doors lead to the courtyard garden, which must be where the apartment is. She is figuring out a way to get in. *Surely she's not.* Yes, she is. I know her. Nancy Reagan's best friend who sits up straight and wears Chanel and advises my father on the illegality of his phone-taping will have no problem trespassing, traipsing over bushes, just to lay eyes on the location of the possible next chapter of my new life. Though she is a rules-follower, she is also a "can do" person. And, between the two, the "can do" usually wins.

"Mom, we can't."

But she isn't listening; she is standing over by the glass doors. I glance back to the attendant who is talking to a group of young women he has just let into the building. I turn back around but my mother is nowhere to be seen.

Five minutes later, I find her in the courtyard. There are daffodils, a pebbled walkway. "You think it's that one, over there?" My mother rushes over to the only small patio off one of the apartments. I am still in disbelief we're doing this, and yet, I'm not. She inspects a small iron table and chairs and dusts them off with her monogrammed hankie. "These have had it. You need new cushions." She tries to open the framed doors leading to the empty apartment, but they are locked.

"Mom, we can't break in!"

"Your living room looks nice," she says excitedly, her nose pressed to the glass. "An area rug on that parquet floor, something in blue and white, perfect."

My living room?

I am at another beginning. And like all my beginnings, my mother is with me. It feels bittersweet given why I'm here, even though this isn't a beginning she would have chosen for me, moving into an apartment alone, divorced. But she embraces it with eagerness as if we were picking out my wedding dress. I get swept up in her enthusiasm and look into the apartment through the glass, too.

"Honey, this apartment is going to be beautiful by the time you get done with it."

I don't as much realize what is happening as much as I feel it, an expansion inside of me. My breath moves deeper into my belly. Why have I never known I have so much extra breathing space? Up until now, I was nervous and my breath was always shallow because I didn't want to take up too much space, as if taking more than my fair share of air would deprive someone more deserving of it. As we turn to walk back out of the courtyard, dusk begins to fall. I am a little sad, but at the same time, a little more free.

30

As I arrive for work the next day carrying a newspaper, I stop by Pam's office to tell her about the apartment. Pam is behind her desk drinking coffee from her ERA mug, reading the *New York Times*. With her polished pale-pink nails, she looks ready to greet the day like the Republican feminist that she is.

Pam glances up at me. Typical for her, she reads my face immediately. "What?" That's all she says. That means, "I know you want to tell me something you're excited about."

I plop down in a chair across from her desk. "How did you find your first apartment?" I'm curious about how others have found their homes if not through signboards.

"Why are you asking?" Pam asks playfully, though it's as if she's read my mind so she doesn't really need an answer.

She thinks for a minute and says, "The classifieds." Then she appears to double-check her memory. "No, through a friend. Long time ago." She laughs.

We stand over Pam's desk, now with my copy of the *New York Times*—open to the classifieds—spread out in front of us. I want to make sure I have other apartment options, in case I don't get the one I saw with my mother. Pam and I circle listings that might be suited to me. She instructs me about a real-estate code: "cozy" means crappy, "unique" means ugly, "charm" means peeling paint and a rusty sink. I want to write all this down but she is talking so fast, and I am so amazed by this whole idea of a world I know nothing about that I barely have time to take it all in.

"And make sure they don't stick you with first and last month's rent up front *and* a security deposit. Got it?" I can tell that she's genuinely happy for me.

I watch her expression; it's as though she is vicariously living through me and, at the same time, cheering me on to live for myself. Sometimes I think Pam knows me better than I know myself. She seems to know the person I am going to be, even when I can't see it.

She cheers me on in a way that my parents can't. And, for a brief second, I wonder if I haven't simply replaced them with someone new to show me the way.

* * *

A FEW DAYS LATER, I SIGN THE LEASE FOR THE APARTMENT I saw with my mother, and I can't wait to tell Pam, to give her all the details. I find her in her office, buried in paperwork for a client. She is seated on her sofa with documents spread out in front of her.

"Pam! I got it," I say loudly.

Pam looks up from her work, a giant smile spreads across her face.

"We have work to do!" she says, enthusiastically.

"We'll start Saturday!"

"Perfect!"

31

"This is so Nancy Reagan." The tone in Pam's voice lets me know that this is not necessarily a good thing.

We are in the bedding section of Hecht's department store in Silver Spring, Maryland, staring at a bed made up with a pattern of tiny birds and flowers. The pattern is genteel, like my parents' bedroom in California.

"Yes, so Royal Reagan," I say, imitating Pam's disparaging tone and quite pleased with myself at the new term I've just invented.

I still care deeply for the Reagans. I'm not coming down on them as people. And I bet my mother wouldn't love my new "Royal" term. Still, it feels good to be with someone closer to my age for a change. Pam steps over to a bed made up with sheets in a colorful, abstract, geometric print. The pattern is right out of the Museum of Modern Art. "This is 'now' and youthful, see?"

I glance back at the pattern of tiny birds and flowers. I don't want to admit to Pam that had she not been here, I would in fact have chosen these very serious sheets. But now when I look at them a second time, I hear Baroque music, staid and proper. How odd.

All this bed linen in front of me makes me think of sex and how I hardly ever had an orgasm with Robin. He would tell me "this is boring" when he got tired of trying to make me climax. It was exhausting for us both. I was so in my head, so nervous. I look back at the geometric pattern and I think, climax. As I stare at the colors and shapes, they sort of dance across the bed like jazz, fiery and fun. I almost hear the beat of the rhythm. I look back at the proper tiny birds and flowers and think, no climax. I wonder if I will ever have great sex, and I get embarrassed, as if I had just announced my thoughts over the department store intercom. I look back at the geometric print again. I start to smile. Pam just gave me permission to be different. It is the strangest thing. I don't have to do what I think I *should* do. I can do what I want and I can give permission to myself.

Jazzy and cool. Me? Why not? What will my mother think? Honestly, she can think what she wants.

* * *

MOVING OUT HAS CHANGED ME IN WAYS I HADN'T IMAGINED. At first, I was excited about having a space of my own, owning furniture. But as the weeks go by, I feel a new sense of what is possible. It's no longer all about using my wedding china, what kind of monogrammed note cards to write on, what to serve Robin's parents when they come over for dinner. I am now an audience of one. I have a sky full of choices, of yeses and noes and maybes. I get to define who I am—or to change who I am, and that feels unlimited.

One night, after a few glasses of wine, alone in my apartment, I break into a comedy routine. In college I had a routine in the dorms; I impersonated a housewife in a Tide laundry commercial. I never forgot the sound of that laughter. Granted, this was in front of six hungover university students. Now, standing in front of my bathroom mirror, I am hysterical. I belt out my words in my best southern accent. "I can get little Johnny's football jersey's clean, with Tide's enzyme-eating action!" People always told me I was funny. I must have inherited the laugh gene from my father. But funny got buried when I got married.

I stuffed funny inside. Now, it feels good to remember that I can be *comedic!*

I see my parents from time to time, but not everything is so serious anymore. I am no longer reading their faces for encouragement or disapproval, no longer living as an appendage to my mother, no longer wandering with Cody the Doberman through *their* house, wondering about *my* life.

Mostly, I spend my time hanging out with Pam. With her, there are no somber dinners sitting up straight while properly holding my fork, politely cutting my chicken one bite at a time as I've been taught, or listening to the latest newspaper article about my father, the drama unfolding like a bad movie. There are no lawyers, no constant calls from the media, no watching Mom clutching the phone, frantically whispering to Nancy Reagan. I can laugh as loud as I want. I can guffaw in the most unattractive way possible, my mouth open wide, my placid politeness replaced by a spontaneous storm.

And, little by little, a new sensation replaces the fear I've always known. It is a softening, a releasing. A kind of "allowing" is how it feels. I'm not anticipating the next bad thing. I am tasting a morsel of peace.

As the weeks go by, Pam and I venture out. We attend exhibits at the National Gallery of Art, listen to book readings in DuPont Circle, eat eggs Benedict at Martin's Tavern in Georgetown, devour pecan pie at Clyde's on M Street. Pam even introduces me to Tom Collins—the sugary rum drink, not the man.

Pam has such a busy life, but somehow she always manages to be there when I need her. She answers the phone when I am lonely, gets me out of the house when I'm feeling down, and even secretly helps me out at work. I still feel behind in my career compared to others my age, and what might seem like common-sense knowledge to them usually has not fully sunk in for me.

"What's on your agenda today?"

I pull out a legal pad with my schedule scribbled on the page.

Pam stares at the pad. "How can you keep your life on that?" She chides me like an older sister looking out for me.

It has never occurred to me to use anything different. This is how I keep my day: I check off one appointment after the next. No doubt it is kind of a mess.

Pam picks up a small notebook off her desk. Black alligator leather, a clasp on the side, with a small strip of leather that snaps shut.

"*This* is a calendar." She hands it to me. "Go ahead, open it."

I unsnap the clasp, touching the small-sized paper; it's thin and delicate.

"It's called a Filofax. My whole life's inside. If I were on the Titanic, this would go in the lifeboat first." Pam laughs, sipping her coffee.

I flip through her appointments, to-do lists, her contacts. It is organized and almost peaceful.

"You *must* have one." Pam tells me they sell them at Garfinckel's.

I like the little notebook. It feels good in my hands. It would be nice to contain my chaos in a luxurious little book. It feels important, imagining my appointments worthy of documentation in leather. Would this be telling myself that I am important, too?

A few days later, Pam overhears me with a client in the hallway. The man asks me the date of an upcoming committee meeting. I falter, ramble, "I'm sorry, I just don't know...I should know."

Pam pulls me inside her office.

"Did I screw that up?" I ask her.

"When you don't know the answer to something, you say, 'I'll look into that; I'll get back to you.'"

It is so simple. But I need help with simple.

A few days later Pam tells me about a difficult client meeting she had. She says he was always demanding and intimidating and wouldn't listen to her.

"I look him in the eye and in the most firm, loving way, I say, 'Bruce, remember, your win is ours. And we never lose.'"

"Just like that?"

"Yup. He never questioned me again."

Wow, I think to myself, *she did that?* So boldly? Could I someday say something like that?

Pam is a feminist, and part of that means not being afraid to stand up to the good ol' boys. I can't help but admire her spunk. But being her friend doesn't necessarily mean that she agrees with me. Little by little I notice signs that indicate that she doesn't quite agree with the way I was brought up.

One night I am in the kitchen, making us drinks, when I hear her shriek. I race into the living room to see what is wrong.

"What is this?!" She is holding up my copy of the *Congressional Club Cook Book.* She looks shocked and overjoyed at the same time. I'm not quite sure what she's thinking. "Where did you get this?" she asks me seriously.

"I got it from my mother-in-law. A gift."

She picks a page at random and begins to read out loud. "Mrs. Olin Teague, wife of former representative from Texas. 'Christmas Shrimp. Y'all need one pound deveined shrimp, two cans of cream of celery soup, two cans of cream of mushroom soup, green pepper, frozen peas, and diced celery.'" Pam looks up at me, a little more serious now. "What *is* this book?"

"It's a book of recipes submitted by wives of congressmen, spouses, friends, and family. It has recipes of entrees, soups, and desserts, each divided by section."

I had never thought about the recipes before or how the women came across. It was a book that everyone I knew had on their shelves. My mother has a copy. As does Mrs. R.

Pam flips through the pages. "Mrs. Donald Brotzman, Mrs. Gerald P. Nye, Mrs. Hamer H. Budge." Can you believe it? As if the women don't deserve their own identities." Pam finds something on one of the pages that makes her laugh.

"Jell-O pinwheel marshmallow mold. Blend together one-fourth jar marshmallow sauce, one cherry and one peach Jell-O packet."

Pam bursts out laughing, which cracks me up, and I start to laugh, too.

"Do another," I request, and Pam stands up straight with one arm behind her back and speaks in a Boston accent, rolling off the ingredients for a Boston cream pie. "Five cups of sugar, three eggs, half a cup of flour."

I'm getting into the spirit of this now and want to be part of the action. "Let me do one!" I want to laugh at the absurdity of it all, and revel in the feeling of seeing the world from a whole new point of view.

"So do you want to do Mrs. Harold S. Sawyer or Mrs. John C. Kunkel?"

She hands me the book and I read out loud. "Mrs. John C. Kunkel. Pennsylvania. Pineapple Cream Cheese Ball. Two eight-ounce packages of cream cheese, one eight and a half cans of crushed pineapple, one quarter cup chopped green pepper, two tablespoons chopped onion, one cup chopped pecan crackers."

We are now in hysterics. Pam is laughing so hard, she might fall off my sofa. I am struck by the feeling of how much I have enjoyed discarding the expectations my parents have of me. Going with the emotion, I toss the cookbook in the trash. I realize the repercussions: This means I will no longer have a recipe for Tuna Boats or Jell-O Pinwheel Marshmallow Mold or the perfect pot roast. No-Crust Pecan Pie will never be a part of my perfect dinner party. That's okay; Chinese takeout is more my style, anyway.

32

"Nancy, do you know where Pam is?" I can't seem to find her anywhere.

"She's out," Nancy smiles, with her blonde hair and dazzling self. She's rushing to a meeting.

I want to tell Pam about this article I just read in the *Times*, a piece about Gloria Steinem, though I'm sure Pam's already seen it. I know that Pam's busy, but it seems I always have something to tell her, to ask her. And she never makes me feel like my visits are an imposition.

"Do you know when she'll be back?"

Nancy is at the end of the hallway now. She shakes her head and disappears around a corner.

The next day Pam isn't in her office again. It's normal for us to go a day without talking, but it seems odd that she'd take two days off work without mentioning it. Her desk is empty, and for a brief instant, her vacant chair feels like a sign. I tell myself I'm being ridiculous. Still, when I run into an assistant in the kitchen, I can't help but ask if she knows anything about Pam.

"Time off" is her evasive answer.

I brush my worry off and head back to my office, trying to concentrate on the long list of tasks that I have to get done.

Over the next few days, I hear nothing. Pam isn't at work, and all anyone says is "She's out," usually accompanied by a chipper, business-friendly smile that is starting to drive me crazy. I dial Pam's number once a day at first, then I start calling more often. On Tuesday, I ring her three times, on Wednesday eight, on Thursday the same. But she never picks up.

One time I even try at night. I don't want to wake her up, but I can't stand not knowing. I figure that if she doesn't answer at three in the morning, she obviously isn't home. The phone rings and rings and rings until finally I stop trying.

Why doesn't she answer her phone? She must know I wonder where she is, that I'm starting to become concerned. *We're close.* You tell your friend, if you're not going to be around. I'm annoyed, suddenly. The more I think about this, the angrier I get. I wouldn't do this to *her*. What is it that she isn't telling me?

33

Finally, five days later, I find Pam in her office.

"Knock, knock."

She looks up from her desk.

"Oh, hey." She seems tired, like she hasn't slept. For a brief instant I feel guilty about my three a.m. phone call. But she probably wasn't home that night anyway.

I don't know what to say. I always felt like we told each other everything, and now I feel a distance, maybe even a slight sense of betrayal. Even now, it seems like she doesn't want to talk, but she tells me, nonchalantly, "Bad back."

I am relieved it isn't anything serious; she had me worried.

She smiles and rolls her eyes as if it's no big deal, as if this was nothing more than a paper cut.

So that's why she's been out. Why didn't she just call and tell me?

"Does it hurt? I'm sorry."

"A bit."

I ask if she wants to go to lunch, and offer to bring us salads if it's hard for her to get around. I'll do anything to get us back to normal and make everything okay. I can pick up sandwiches if she prefers. How about Thai food? A great place just opened three blocks away. Their green curry is to die for.

I hold my breath, waiting. Should I have suggested Italian?

"That's so nice of you to offer, but I have to lunch with the partners. You know how that is."

Is she blowing me off? No, she is having a work lunch, she just said that. But there is something in her tone that increases my discomfort. Did I do something to upset her?

34

When my mother gets angry, she gets quiet. She grew up with Midwestern restraint—calm and controlled. She is ladylike.

I was never sure how to deal with so much silence. She would walk into the kitchen, eyes wide, lips pursed; she'd walk past me as if I wasn't there. That meant she was angry. One time when I was in the kitchen, she came in and started searching the cabinets for something, banging them shut, like she was making sure the hinges were fastened. But I knew this was her anger, since she never felt entitled to express it. I didn't say anything because I also knew it was pointless. If I asked her whether she was upset, she'd just say, "No, not at all." There was nothing I could do and I'd wish she would just tell me what I had done, to get it out in the open. That way I could apologize or explain. Not knowing was what drove me crazy. It was impossible to fix what I didn't understand.

I figure there must be some clue in my calendar to help me understand what I've done wrong with Pam. On a mission now, I take out my Filofax from my top office drawer and scrutinize the events of last week. Staff meeting on March 2nd. That was when I accidentally interrupted Pam. She was talking about the date for our Railroad client call, and before she could finish, I said, "March 30th." I finished her sentence when I didn't have to, and I don't know why I did that. I had felt bad then, I remember. Still, we talked on the way out and everything seemed okay. Pam even offered me a bite of her pastry.

On March 4th, at the Motion Picture Association meeting at two p.m., I laughed at something Anne Wexler said. I noticed Pam wasn't laughing and when I caught her eye she didn't acknowledge me. Or maybe it was a few days later when I said I had met Jack Valenti with my parents? I told everyone. Did I come off as bragging? But Pam tells me to *own* who I meet. I continue my way through the Filofax. It is just a bunch of dates and times and meetings, but each one makes me recall some faux pas I made, some blunder that no one else would have committed. Pam could be angry about what I did on any one of those days, or maybe it is just the cumulative effect of all of my mistakes put together.

I decide to write Pam a note. A note will let me say what I'm too nervous to say out loud. My mother has always written elegant notes expressing her thoughts. On her personalized note cards, she wishes happy birthday, merry Christmas, sorry for your loss. It's so respect-able—her words penned down neatly on the stock card, sometimes in red ink. She says on paper what she might say out loud, yet the act of writing the words immortalizes them somehow. These words are anchored.

I'm on my last carton of Ben & Jerry's, sitting at my dining table. I wipe the chocolate off my hands, and I walk to my hall closet. I hunt for a box of my stationery. I'll explain how I feel, apologize for all of the stupid things I did over the past week. I'll make her comfortable. Let her know she's not stuck with me as a friend, that I don't mean to glom on, and I appreciate so much all she's done for me. Something like that. Good. A classy note on my personal, classy stationary. I open the box. Cream paper with my name engraved in red lettering. There is some-thing affirming about this stationery, something regal—safe, even. This stationery says to people, "There is something important written on this paper. Surely you'll take the time to read this missive fully."

I run my fingers over the red letters of my name. And then I stop. Because it's not my name. Why hadn't I thought of this? The name at the top of the paper is not Pam Wick. The lettering reads "Mrs. Robin Michel." How many thank-you notes did I write on this stationary? Hundreds. "Dear X, thank you for the fancy Crock-Pot." "Dear Y, we just love the engraved picture frames." How many times did I use this stationery to say what was expected, having no idea how I really felt?

I decide not to write Pam a note after all. At this moment everything just feels so insincere.

35

I have almost convinced myself that Pam is never going to call me again when the phone suddenly rings. I'm getting ready for work, and I race to pick up the receiver.

"Pam!" I shout into the receiver when I hear her voice. I'm filled with a sense of relief.

"Sorry I haven't called."

"It's okay." I say the words, but suddenly I don't mean them. I am angry and I have the right to be. I thought we were friends. What could possibly be so important that made Pam disappear for five days, without so much as a warning phone call?

"It's my back," Pam says by way of explanation. Her voice sounds wobbly, as if she's afraid. This worries me. I had never considered that she might be seriously sick or hurt. I listen as she tells me she's going into the hospital.

"Hopefully it's not a big deal."

I think about the moment she told me about her back. I thought I had seen a cane by the door, but I hadn't registered it in my mind. Why didn't I ask her about it then? I realize this was never about me. Pam was not annoyed at anything I did. I feel relieved and, at the same time, very concerned for her.

"I should return to work soon."

"What's wrong with your back?"

"They're going to fix it. I have a problem; it's messed up."

I'm worried. As if Pam senses this, she continues.

"It's no big deal, honestly."

Still, I can't stop worrying.

36

I can't decide whether Pam's issue is nothing or if I should be concerned. If she didn't even mention the problem with her spine at first, then maybe she's not telling me the full story now. What I need is solid information, facts that give me the full picture. I get my chance later that day when Nancy Reynolds and I are meeting Mrs. Bush to show her the final promo for the PBS *Reading Rainbow* program. We are in Nancy's car, a heavy spring downpour pelting the roof; Connecticut Avenue is drenched in rain. I turn to her, her manicured hands gripping the wheel.

"Nancy," I start, nervously.

"Uh huh?"

"I heard from Pam this morning."

"Good."

"Yeah, it was nice to talk to her."

"Sure, I bet it was."

Nancy offers a quick smile. But the tone in her voice feels kind of forced.

"So, I'm wondering about her," I finally say.

"I can understand that."

"She's going into the hospital, she told me."

Nancy doesn't respond at first.

Then she glances over at me.

"I think it would cheer you up if you visit."

That's all she says.

The sound of the windshield wipers *wish-washes* and the rain thumps on the roof of the car. I tell myself that everything is going to be fine, but deep down I can't help but fear the worst.

37

The Columbia Hospital for Women is a grand terracotta brick structure with a Spanish tile roof and two adjacent wings. Like so many buildings in Washington, it has a story to tell. It was originally built as a healthcare facility for wives and widows of Civil War soldiers. I imagine women, their husbands dying on the bloody battlefield, wondering about how they will get on with their lives.

It's close to noon when I arrive to see Pam. My tote bag is stuffed with some work files, which she requested, and a bouquet of peonies in my hand. I walk across the large, circular, grassy driveway. As I step through the double glass doors and into the hospital, I am hit by crisp and cold air-conditioning and the smell of cleaning fluid—antiseptic, bitter pine, lemon, and bleach. The noises are a patchwork of sounds: announcements over the intercom; the voices of doctors, nurses, and visitors; low mumbles; and loud directives. The gift shop window is filled with flowers, balloons, and stuffed animals. This is a world unto itself, where people try to heal.

I reach the main reception desk and ask to be directed to Pam's room. The nurse tells me third floor, Room 226. I am finally going to see her, and I am excited. I reach Pam and find her flat on her back, pearls resting on top of her hospital gown. A few get-well cards are kept on her bedside table.

"Hi!" she says cheerfully, in spite of the fact that she is in pain.

I am so happy to see her! I rush over to her bed and try to give her a hug, which is awkward because she can't lift her arms. I notice Pam can't move.

"Sorry, surgery rod, can't sit up."

Pam had surgery to insert a metal rod into her back to provide support for her spine, she tells me. She has small fractures in her back, and the rod will stabilize her bones.

I take in my surroundings—the private room, trees outside through the windows.

"There's a vase in the bathroom. Peonies, my fave. Thank you."

I am smiling. I'm just so happy to see Pam. I can't wait till she's better, I tell her.

"We have to go for Tom Collinses, and there's a sale at Garfinckel's." Even though we are in the hospital it feels like old times. As I fill the vase in her bathroom, I take in a big breath of air, as if I've been holding my breath for days. I spot Pam's monogrammed robe on the door. I am momentarily amused. It's like she's at the Four Seasons.

"I heard you and Nancy met with Barbara Bush on the *Reading Rainbow* promo. Nancy said it went well," Pam says from her bed.

"It went great; Mrs. Bush is so nice," I continue, as I walk back into her room with the flowers.

"Did Nancy tell you? The promo references this episode called 'Feelings.' Nothing to do with that cheesy song."

I set the flowers on a table next to a framed photo of Pam from the '70s. I recognize the other two women in the picture from when Pam had shown me this photo before, in her office: Congresswoman Bella Abzug, wearing a hat, and Betty Friedan. A younger Pam is sandwiched in between these courageous women. I imagine this was one of the best moments of her life. No wonder she brought this photo to the hospital.

"God, 'Feelings.' If I never hear that idiot song again I'm good," Pam muses.

"Are you in a lot of pain?" I hope it's okay for me to ask this.

"I'm on a lot of medication. But the worst part is that I have to stare up at this pathetic ceiling all day. That's shitty."

I shove away my thoughts and look up at the ceiling.

"Can't you roll on your side?" I ask.

"Nope. Flat. Like this," she says, imitating a dead body.

"Hmmm...can't turn your head just a little, so you can look sideways?"

"What part of flat on my back are you not understanding?" Pam says, good-naturedly.

"Sorry. Well, it's not a bad ceiling. Those tiles, they're even. Functional."

Pam stares up, frowning, then offers her opinion.

"They need to redo them—they're worn around the edges. This hospital can do better," she says.

We sit for a few moments. The fluorescent lights hum in the background.

Then Pam starts to talk; she sounds frustrated.

"I have work piling up. Did you bring the files? My clients are okay with the backlog. For now. Of course, if I'm out longer, they may not be so understanding. I could be in here for a while. Tests. God-damned tests."

I look at Pam talking to the ceiling. Her usual composure has vanished. For the first time she appears vulnerable. A turquoise plastic water pitcher sits alone on her tray. She is hooked up to a monitor which beeps rhythmically; colorful graphs blink on the screen.

I look back up at the ceiling. Then I involuntarily stand. In one motion, I morph into my comedic self. I pretend to hold a microphone. A rush of adrenalin pushes through me, and I burst into song.

"Ceilings! Ceilings...nothing more than ceilings.

"Trying to forget my ceilings of love...

"Teardrops, rolling down on my face..."

As I continue my terrible rendition of the song, Pam is laughing, so I sing louder.

"Ceilings, whoa, whoa, ceilings...

"Again, in my life..."

She is laughing so hard she lets out a snort. Then finally she mutters through laughter, "Stop, it hurts to laugh."

I plunk down in the guest chair and look over at her. My heart beats in my chest as I recover. It's as if all my love for Pam morphed into some strange brand of humor.

38

I step out of Pam's room brimming with contentment, knowing that my visit indeed cheered her up. I am thankful to Nancy. Relief washes over me again.

I walk down the hall expecting to find the elevator when I realize that I must have taken a wrong turn. I now have no idea where the elevators are, though I am not far from Pam's room; so I ask a doctor in his white lab coat, walking briskly toward me.

"Through oncology, beyond those doors."

I look at him, unsure of his words.

"Oncology?"

He senses my confusion.

"That's where you are."

It can't be possible. This isn't orthopedics? My friend's *here*? And suddenly I know that the worst wasn't all in my imagination. The worst has finally arrived.

I step toward the elevators and have a sense of unreality, as if I'm floating, as if my feet don't touch the antiseptic linoleum floor of the hospital hallway. I feel like I'm walking just above the floor, through a fog of opaqueness. Even the sounds are muffled. How is it that I entered Pam's room filled with optimism?

What does it feel like to be Pam, staring up at the ceiling all day? Why didn't she just tell me? And why did she ask me to bring her files? She can't even sit up; how would she possibly hold them?

In the hospital lobby, I smell the same cleaning fluid and antiseptic as when I entered. I hear the same noises—announcements over the intercom, doctors, nurses. I see the same gift shop window, flowers. But nothing is the same. Everything has been rearranged, including, it seems, my insides. I pass through the hospital doors into the muggy day, which feels damp. Walking back across the large, circular driveway, I carry with me deep sadness, a kind of dislocation, a sense of being lost.

39

At night I can't sleep. All I can think about is Pam. I am filled with anxiety, my mind racing. How is this possible? Am I going to lose her? Thoughts ping-pong in my head. It seems so utterly dire, seeing her again in my mind, on her hospital bed, hooked up to machines, staring at the ceiling. What if she never comes out of the hospital? I feel like I am trapped in an elevator that is falling, with no floor to land on.

I'm reminded of my cousin. Even when we were little, Michael was quiet, his skin was sort of translucent, and I always worried about him. As if to prove my anxiety right, he actually was diagnosed with cancer. I remember when he first got sick; he told me it felt like the flu. He was overwhelmed by the tests he was having to take. Then he went into the hospital.

When I visited him with my mother, we went to the nurse's station to try and get a VHS player in his room so he could watch movies. They didn't have many of these machines at that time. I overheard the nurse talking to another nurse, saying my cousin should get the VHS machine because "he's probably going to die here." I was terrified when I heard that; I couldn't believe it. When the VHS player arrived in his room, I hated looking at it, sitting across from his bed. He was gone a few days later.

Michael had such goodness. He was gentle, and when he talked to you he was fully present. His eyes were kind of watery at times. He laughed when he was amused, a pleasant, rolling sound, that made his shoulders shake in slow motion. He called me Pammy. We used to play hide-and-seek in his backyard near his family house bordering Rancho Park. To think something so violent and aggressive as cancer could take over this gentle person.

My father always told us, "Just remember kids, nothing stays the same."

40

"Nancy, just tell me what's wrong with Pam."

It's as though Pam is in the deep end of the ocean, treading water to stay afloat. "She has cancer." Nancy sits across from me, behind her elegant desk—her enviable Rolodex and a stack of *Congressional Quarterly* magazines nearby. She hesitates, removes her glasses, and sighs visibly, her resting happy face now a frown.

"She has multiple myeloma. It's advanced. We're praying for her."

I learn that Pam has a cancer that starts in the bone marrow. And bone marrow is what helps our bodies fight infections and, generally, makes sure we live healthy lives. In early stages multiple myeloma can be treated and people even go on to live for many years after being diagnosed. Thus, the metal rod in her spine to strengthen the weakened and fractured bones.

While Nancy tells me that Pam could still have a long time left—or at least there exists that possibility—all I can think of is what this diagnosis means. I ignore Nancy's words about good probabilities, lots more productive years, and not giving up hope. Instead I have this overwhelming sense of loneliness.

The realization that people leave hits me. Robin left. My parents got too consumed with their own lives to see me. And now Pam—hers is absolutely tragic, unimaginable.

41

"Hi, there," Pam says weakly from her bed. She is pale, hooked up to machines, flowers on her nightstand. I am afraid. I pretend I'm okay and tell her that I came by because I thought she'd like the company. I ask if she's hungry—as if she would tell me she's craving a BLT, which would make me so happy. I could get her one with mayo and we could chat and figure out plans for the weekend. But she's not hungry; some leftover dinner on a tray near her bed tells me this.

"You can't believe the office," I tell her. "Everyone's scrambling for the congressional telecommunications hearing tomorrow. I'm stapling documents in our conference room. Anne whips through, checking our work. I'm so afraid I'm going to staple page four to page six that I focus like I'm a NASA engineer."

I laugh, hoping Pam is enjoying the story.

But I can tell her mind is elsewhere. I can tell she is exhausted and drugged, overwhelmed by the mountain of thoughts in her head. As she moves slightly, trying to get comfortable, I watch her struggle. Then she says, with a kind of urgency, that she has worked hard and that I need to continue. "You have a voice and you need to use it."

I realize that Pam is saying goodbye. Inside, I collapse onto myself, all of me folding into a little square of terror. I hear her words through a film of fear. I'm going to lose her. Maybe it will be a few weeks, a few months, or even years. But the loneliness is there now.

"Remember...you have to get out there, help all you can." Pam wants to make sure that I will fight for women. She won't allow me *not* to step in for her. *I am not the right person to carry the cause*, I want to say to her. I came to Washington with my Lark suitcases my mother and Nancy Reagan picked out for me, with the stripe down the middle and my married initials embossed in gold. So how will I stand up for women when I am *me*, and when I am always plagued by fear?

Pam's hand looks small no longer clutching her ERA coffee mug. On her wrist, there is a hospital ID bracelet where there once were chunky, gold designer links. The monitors beep in a rhythm that tells me nothing stays the same.

42

"You don't know—she may pull through," my father says, tossing nuts into his mouth. My mother looks over at me. I can tell she's worried; her blonde hair pulled into its customary bun, and in her delicate hand a cut crystal glass with ice, scotch, and soda. My parents are having their nightly cocktails and all I want is for them to make Pam better. I want them to put down their drinks, and for my father to call the head of the National Institutes of Health and get a second opinion for Pam. But I know that all they are able to do is speculate and shine a positive light in the darkness. Posture perfect, my mother is the cover of *Town & Country*: "At home with the Wicks in Washington." However, her glossy exterior appears slightly dulled; there is a flatness to her former shine. Her eyes, typically wide with enthusiasm, look tired; her brow is furrowed and her mouth tense. The months of my father's scandal—the worry and shame—have affected her. I get the sense that she, like me, is engulfed in fear and still can't find her way out.

"Look, you can be sure the doctors are doing everything possible for her," my father says.

"Your job is to remain strong, helping Pam by being a good friend."

When did my parents lose their ability to fix things?

"Darling, life is tough."

My father is unable to comfort me. He is doing everything he can, but I am inconsolable. All he can do is sit before the unpropitious facts and watch them tower over me in his attempt to help.

"Unfortunately, life is full of lessons," my father continues. He tells me he has learned many of them during this year. "We can't control things, we must be accountable for our actions, and"—I've heard this over the years—"to thine own self be true."

Then he looks at me with such love and compassion that for the moment my heart is encircled, my fear dissolving into only love.

43

"Four more years!" is the chant that rings through the convention hall at the Republican National Convention in Dallas. "Four more years!" The place is packed, the energy palpable. Senators, congressmen, and over four thousand delegates gather together to nominate President Reagan for a second term. There is Senator Alan Simpson from Wyoming, Senator Paul Laxalt from Nevada. There are celebrities—actor Arnold Schwarzenegger, singer Ray Charles. It is August, hot, nearly a hundred degrees outside, but that doesn't stop the festivities. The chaos, the lunches, dinners, and cocktails continue late into the evening. Lone Star State Apparel has replaced Brooks Brothers suits and ties. There are folks in cowboy boots, hats, and denim. Lots of power-hobnobbing over chili, lavish barbecues, and tequila.

In spite of the heat, it is a relief to be out of Washington. Six months have passed since Pam became ill and I'm trying to make the best of my new normal. Something I have come to understand is that illness has repercussions beyond the sickness. People pull away. Pam has pulled away. When she is in the office, she remains behind her desk working nonstop for her clients. I bring her salads. I try to be there for her. But there is no room for me. She is only able to be there for herself. She depends on longtime friends and family, and they are there for her.

But here, away from Washington, I am removed from my sadness, and we are nominating our family friend Ronald Reagan for a second presidential term. I feel at peace. My parents are here, and this fills me with a sense of hope—as if the old California days are back. As if my father just decided he could help Ronald Reagan get elected the first time and my parents are invincible once again, and we are all caught up in the possibility of victory. And life, in spite of its reversals, might be okay.

Nancy and I are in the Presidential Sky Suite overlooking the convention floor, an elegant space with couches, a bar, "Reagan-Bush '84" campaign posters, and lots of red, white, and blue décor. I feel energized by the sounds from the floor on this first night. I hear horns and applause. I remember the feeling I had at Laguna Beach, when my family moved us there for a month each summer. On days of our arrival, there was nothing to look forward to but fun. Looking out over the convention floor now, I feel a jolt of joy. It's as if an electric current of hope is pulsing through me, and it occurs to me, unequivocally, that anything is possible.

Although technically I am on the clock, it doesn't feel like it. My job, working alongside Nancy Reynolds, is to oversee the box and host family and friends of the Reagans—as well as a handful of top-tier donors. I actually feel lucky, and as if I belong here. As if I am finally back on the right path in my life. I'm not intimidated, I can talk to pretty much anyone, and my insides are calm.

Nancy introduces me to a young lawyer named Patrick Doyle. "He's our lightening rod to the FCC." (I congratulate myself for knowing the acronym.) I notice Nancy talks to Patrick with a kind of reverence, as if he is important. Patrick, in his khaki suit, is not exactly handsome—a bit thin, yet attractive in a nerdy way. "Patrick worked in presidential personnel. He's a big fan of our president."

"Ron Dog is the best!" Patrick says, and I realize he's talking about Ronald Reagan. I laugh to myself, "Ron Dog"? I can tell he is enjoying all of this as much as I am.

44

Over the next four days there are more lunches, dinners, and cocktails. My favorite time is when I'm hanging out with Nancy and Patrick in our hotel bar, packed with convention-goers. We unwind after long days and mingle over tequila and Dos Equis. One night Patrick brings his hilarious friend Jim Bayless, a Washington lawyer and a good friend of the Bush family. Jim has a Texas twang and no matter what he says, especially after a few drinks, I can't help but howl with laughter.

On one of the nights we are socializing, Jim cracks a joke. "How do we know communism was doomed from the beginning? All the red flags!" He slaps his knee, he's laughing so hard.

I am having so much fun that I'm caught off guard one night when Patrick slips off to the bar to buy us another round of drinks and Jim turns to me. "I'd like to take you out, when we get back to Washington."

I don't know what to say. I haven't even considered dating. It's been nine months since Robin, and, as much as I hate to admit it to myself, I miss being with someone. Not that it was good with him. But at least I wasn't alone. I think about what it would be like to have someone to come home to, someone to laugh with. I look over at Jim, his long, narrow face, his permanent grin, as if he expects me to say "great, I'd love to go out with you.'" All I feel is the warm fondness of friendship. I don't want to lead him on or hurt his feelings.

How do I let him off easy?

"You don't want to date me. I have way too much emotional baggage."

This doesn't seem to deter him. Instead, he looks strangely happy. "Emotional baggage? Uh huh, good...I'd like to help you unpack it." I don't know what to say, so I just laugh along with Jim, hoping he'll fall for another girl in the bar.

45

"Did you hear what Senator Simpson said?" Patrick leans over and I wait for the punch line. "In Washington, DC, the high road of humility is not troubled by heavy traffic!"

I laugh now with the same enthusiasm I had in Texas, except it's better now because we are back in DC. Jim is now long gone (though we promised to stay in touch), Reagan is now the official nominee for the Republican Party, and Mrs. R is no longer holding court in the presidential box—she's back to her First-Lady-Washington duties. Life has moved on since the convention, but the thing that has remained constant is the presence of Patrick in my life.

Now we are at a Mexican restaurant near the Capitol enjoying too many margueritas.

"So, here's one," I continue. "How d'you know when it's really cold in Washington, DC? When politicians put their hands in their own pockets!"

There is an ease between Patrick and me, and I think maybe it's that we're both from Southern California. Patrick and I both love the tiny bit of rain in January out west, when the skies are overcast and the plants are happy to drink it all up, while in other places people love the sun. It almost feels like we knew each other growing up.

As he sits across from me I notice his face is slightly weathered, as if he baked in the California sun too many times. "Did you ever imagine you'd wind up in Washington?"

I think about it for a minute and tell him no, I was never into politics.

He studies my face. "But your family, and the Reagans. How could you *not* want to be *here*?"

"I'm starting to like it," I say. I wonder, *am I*? I am enjoying this now, I realize. Sitting here, across from Patrick. Then a surprising warmth sweeps over me. I feel happy in this moment. It's been so long since I felt this, I try to hold onto it.

He looks at me, his grey-green eyes searching, as if he's about to say something I need to hear. "We can change the world. This is our opportunity." He cracks his knuckles as if this thought is almost too much, too thrilling. What is he saying? I've never considered something so big. I am a little bit intimidated. What a responsibility, to change the world? Yet, I envy his passion.

As we reminisce about the convention, I ask, "How's that girl from the bar in Dallas?"

The whole time at the convention, Patrick was chatting up this girl with long legs and long, dark hair. She struck me as bubbly and engaging. I could tell he really liked her, and Jim and I teased him about it.

He looks off, considering. He explains that they got along at first, but he realized that she was basically not sold on our president. "She doesn't like his environmental policies. So why was she at the convention?" he asks me, as if I know the answer. Patrick pops a taco chip into his mouth as he mulls this over. I feel his intensity as he tells me how he felt she was not someone he could be with. "She was basically disloyal to Ron Dog." He seems distressed. For a second it seems an odd reason to break up with someone, but then I realize it has to do with his conviction, his passion, and his loyalty to President Reagan.

I glance at Patrick's slim wrists poking out from under the cuffs of his Oxford cloth button-down shirt, holding a glass across the table. I have such a good friend in him, and I am so grateful. I feel like maybe he's kind of like Pam. They're different, and yet they both make me feel seen.

46

"William Webster, Director of the FBI? He was recently widowed," my mother says, as if this should provoke my interest. She promises to introduce us as soon as she spots him.

My parents have talked me into going to a dinner dance at the Canadian Embassy. I have put on a black, designer skirt. It is a voluminous cascade created from Irish linen. The designer, Sybil Connolly, was a favorite of Jackie Kennedy. Jackie wore a Connolly gown in her official White House portrait.

I have prepared myself for the evening ahead. I've managed to learn about the Canadian ambassador, and I plan to say a few words to him about our client—the New York Power Authority—and their interest in Canadian hydropower. That will hopefully make the entrée for a meeting with my bosses. I plan to sound like I know what I'm talking about. What I haven't counted on is my mother trying to be a matchmaker.

William Webster? He's, like, sixty. I can't believe it. But yes, I can, actually. My mother feels that my future is to be the wife of a prominent man, and there is an opening as I am single. I believe she'd like me to waltz up to William Webster in my giant skirt, charm him, and claim a dignified, magazine-cover life. Forget about the thirty-year age difference.

But I'm not interested in an eligible man decades older than I am.

As I watch Ambassador Allan Gotlieb and his wife Sondra greet guests in the elegant entryway with polished marble floors and tapestry rugs, I think what a perfect couple they make. I read that they got married in Winnipeg after only nine dates. She was eighteen, he was twenty-six. I bet she'd never consider marrying someone thirty years older than herself. How could my mother even mention William Webster?

I don't have the courage to speak to the ambassador in the first half hour of cocktails. Maybe it's because he holds court in the corner of the living room, surrounded by important-looking men and a few important-looking women. I'd have to elbow my way in, in my voluminous skirt, and I imagine they'd politely elbow me out of the way. It occurs to me that they must need something from Ambassador Gotlieb, or maybe he needs something from them. I realize I am no different. This is Washington, and though the trappings are tasteful and the champagne flows freely, the room is pure elbow grease and hard work, with intermittent fun.

My father *is* the fun. He always has been. I've never known anyone who worked harder, accomplished so much, and at the same time knows how to tell a good joke or argue a point. Dad is now at the piano playing "O Canada!" Democratic Senator Edward Zorinsky of Nebraska sings along, as does Republican Senator Nancy Landon Kassebaum of Kansas. Dad's attorney Len Garment accompanies him on the saxophone.

I watch from my seat on a sofa. Senator Nancy Kassebaum reminds me of Pam. Short, wavy hair, totally confident. An equal among men. Pam would love being here. She would immediately know whom to meet first and never sit by herself on the sofa. She'd circulate, be interested, and create rapport—all in her pearls. Then she'd write five call reports with follow-up action items for each of them on Monday before lunch.

So, I slowly stand up and step toward the crowd in the direction of Ambassador Gotlieb.

As I do, I hear my name being called and I turn to see a woman talking with my mother. They motion me over.

"Pam, you remember Buffy Cafritz," Mom says.

I greet Buffy, a glamorous, red-haired woman in a flashy gold gown.

"William Webster, Director of the FBI." Buffy motions to a dark-haired man standing next to her.

I look at my mother. She nods approvingly.

Am I missing something? I'm in my twenties. He could be my father.

I excuse myself and slowly step across the room, feeling slightly proud. Instead of remaining with my mother and Buffy and considering William Webster, I choose to do my job. I walk toward Ambassador Gotlieb, who is actually alone in the entryway, when a grey-haired man in a velvet blazer steps in front of me. He takes the ambassador's arm and I realize I missed my small window of opportunity. I don't know what to do.

I look back at William Webster and notice him still talking with the group of men. I wonder just for a minute what it might be like to be married to him. Mrs. FBI? He *is* handsome—dark hair, tailored suit. He's not really old-looking. I imagine I'd have an intriguing life. Would it be dangerous? Would we have dinner with informants? I imagine my future life as an episode from *The F.B.I.* series. It would be like being married to Inspector Lewis Erskine, with a new case each week and someone always getting shot. The whole idea is ridiculous.

I'm jarred out of my thoughts when I notice William Webster walking toward *me*. He makes eye contact. I feel he must know who I am. Is he coming to talk to me? Does he know my mother is trying to set us up? Is he in on this ridiculous plan of hers? I panic and quickly turn to Ambassador Gotlieb, still in conversation with the grey-haired man.

"Sorry to interrupt, but I have a small piece of business to discuss with the ambassador." I take the ambassador's arm just as I'd seen the man do before me. The grey-haired man looks confused as Ambassador Gotlieb turns to me. He smiles, bemused, a drink in one hand.

I realize I haven't planned out what I want to say. My mind draws a blank. So I motion toward the painting hanging above an antique table near us.

"French, 19th century. Is that a Tissot? I wrote my thesis on French painting and poetry at Berkeley. Next to Alfred Stevens and Monet... Tissot was a genius!"

Ambassador Gotlieb's face lights up. He pulls me closer to the masterpiece.

"I am so delighted you appreciate art. You're a kindred spirit. You know, I also attended Berkeley," he tells me.

"Go Bears!" I high-five the ambassador.

He stifles a laugh and all of a sudden William Webster is standing next to me. I am alarmed, fearing my mother told him about her eldest daughter. I worry that he has the wrong idea. What if he asks me out? It's one thing to turn down Patrick's pal Jim, but the head of the FBI? How could I tell him I have too much emotional baggage?

Webster gives me an obligatory smile, and he takes the ambassador's arm, just as I had, and the grey-haired man before me had. Ambassador Gotlieb winks at me as I back away.

I think about William Webster and how when I'm forty, he'll be seventy. What *was* my mother thinking?

47

After the formality and seriousness of the party at the Canadian Embassy, it's a relief to be with Patrick again. It's also nice to be with a crowd where the average age doesn't hover around sixty.

Although I'm not necessarily interested in our hosts, the National Association of Broadcasters (NAB), it just feels good to be out. As we mingle in the Capital Hilton banquet room, two blocks from the White House, Patrick turns to me.

"You look great." He admires my Chanel knock-off suit my mother found for me at Saks. He looks great, too. He usually looks too thin. Maybe it's his suit—it fits well. Or maybe it's that knowing him makes me look past his imperfections.

Patrick introduces me to the president of the NAB, a lively Southerner. "This is Pam Wick."

Ed Fritts looks at me, pauses, then asks, "Are you any relation to Charlie Wick?"

"I'm his daughter."

"I love Charlie Wick. Your dad and the president, doing a great job on this Voice of America deal."

Ed proceeds to describe how President Reagan and my father want to create a radio station to broadcast news to Cuba from the States, to give citizens of the communist country access to American news.

However, Castro hates this idea, and when he found out about it, he retaliated by jamming multiple US radio stations.

"Fortunately, we found a solution," Fritts says, congratulating himself, grinning. Then he explains that a compromise was reached in Congress, and Radio Martí, the US station, became a part of the Voice of America. "Results are pretty much the same, but this is less threatening to Castro."

I know all of this already from my father. Still, I'm not sure what to say in response. "Right, right." But what I'm really struck by is that he has not once referred to Dad's taping scandal. No "Gee, sorry about your dad, he's still a good guy." It is a huge relief. I remind myself that the House Foreign Affairs Committee has completed its investigation of my father with no punitive action. The district attorney in Florida (where Dad taped from) declined to prosecute because they felt it was not warranted, and my father was cleared by a Los Angeles grand jury of any felony charges.

"I want to meet Charlie Wick," Patrick chirps up. I think of the two of them and how similar they are. I'm sure they would get along. My father would love that Patrick is a smart lawyer and a Reagan loyalist.

"That would be great," I say, and as I do, Patrick puts his arm around my waist. It's so natural, so much like the automated way that you extend your hand in greeting when meeting someone for the first time. So, I try not to put too much weight on it.

I don't say anything as Patrick continues talking to Fritts using words like "license holding," "fairness doctrine," and "station ownership," all while keeping his arm around my waist, like it belongs there.

Later, we walk out onto 16th Street. The night air feels cool. Patrick takes my hand, and now I *know* that this is nothing like a handshake. I am surprised that it feels like the most natural thing in the world.

48

The aroma of a fresh brew is a pause, an invitation to slow down and sip the rich, dark, warm liquid. It greets me in the morning, when I'm groggy, coaxing me to start my day. Coffee is always with me as I read the paper. No matter what the headline, coffee comforts me. Its rich smell and flavor, its bold notes rival the fickle, capricious news of the day. Long after the stories fade, long after the fallout from events, coffee remains. It shows up daily like a good friend. Whether in my kitchen or in a café, the aroma of coffee tells me I am safe.

Even as a kid before I started drinking coffee, I loved the whiff of fresh brew. As I would practice piano lessons before school, coffee brewing in our kitchen would make its way to my nose. A bit later, without fail, my father would walk into our living room, pause briefly, then come over to me. He would then set his cup of coffee on the piano and help me with my lesson. I loved the rattle of his cup on its saucer as he placed it down. I knew this signaled that he would calmly, lovingly demonstrate how to properly play a chord. I was always grateful because inevitably I was challenged. Coffee meant help was on the way.

I smell it even before I enter the office kitchen. I anticipate coffee's rich taste, signaling the start of a workday. As I enter, I see Bob Schule at the counter, staring down at an empty coffee mug in his hands. He's not moving, just standing, as if frozen in thought. I'm about to say something. Then I realize he is holding Pam's ERA coffee mug. It must have been in the cabinet. Pam is not in this week, which so often happens.

I don't know what to say; I am under a blanket of grief, with the crushing way Bob looks up at me.

"Kills, just kills me," he says softly.

I reach out and put my arm over his shoulder. We stand together, the smell of fresh-brewing coffee. I try to hold on to the good feeling that coffee always brings.

49

The rest of the day, I walk around as if in a dream—the kind of dream where I don't understand where I am. There is a sense of disassociation as I sit in our staff meeting. I hear the voices but don't comprehend what they're saying, as if I am in slow motion and everything else is in normal speed. I can't seem to catch up. How can this be happening? It's been eight months since Pam got sick. Did I just bury my sadness? Not feel it enough? Did I leave some inside me and now it is bubbling up? Or does it simply return until it wears you down so that you become less of who you were before, forever altered by the sickness of a beloved friend?

By the afternoon I begin to feel afraid, though I'm not sure when exactly or why the sensation shifts. In a meeting with Anne, I start to panic. One minute I am taking notes about hydroelectric energy, and the next minute I'm breaking out in a cold sweat.

I have to excuse myself. I rush into the hallway, take deep breaths, and wait for it to pass. I'm no stranger to panic and this feeling is familiar, but this is more ominous. It is mixed with crushing loss. I am so afraid. Then the thoughts go through my head like they so often to do. Maybe she will be okay? She'll get better. They'll find a cure. But she is not getting better. All I can think about is the quote from C.S. Lewis I read in college: "No one ever told me that grief felt so like fear." At the time, I was frustrated that I didn't understand the quote. Now I am frustrated that I do.

I hope that I will feel better once I am in the safety of my apartment, but at night I can't sleep. I sit up in bed and stare out the window into the garden. I spot a single light from another window across the courtyard. Is this where we meet, those of us in fear, at night when we can't sleep? Staring out into the darkness at each other's windows? Hoping that by seeing a window with a light on, we can share and lessen our grief?

50

"I'm taking you someplace special." Patrick is behind the wheel as we drive along the Potomac. Cotton-ball clouds fill the sky; autumn light floods the landscape. In the back of the car is a picnic he prepared. Patrick seems happy behind the wheel, chatting about his love of Indian summer. I want to join his good mood but I feel uneasy somehow, as if the sun isn't really shining, and I am coated in an opaque sadness.

He stops the car under the canopy of a vast oak tree somewhere in the Virginia countryside. Patrick carries the picnic basket from the back and I realize that I have also gotten out of the car without actually thinking about it. He places the blanket on the grass and I force myself to get out of my head. Glancing down at the colorful blanket, I smile at the picnic. It's a still life—crusty bread sandwiches, purple grapes, apples. If only I can rest peacefully in this moment I can be happy. There is nothing in this singular instant that is upsetting or that can threaten me, I tell myself. We remove our shoes and the warm sunshine feels reassuring. A ladybug crawls along my arm. It's Nancy Reagan red, I think to myself. Patrick tells me to make a wish. Amidst the sweet smell of dandelions and buzzing of tiny insects, I silently ask for everything bad to go away.

Patrick looks at me with tenderness; I can tell he senses I'm sad. I feel bad; I'm spoiling our day. I've only been fun up till now. I'm so afraid he won't understand why I'm sad and even if he says he does, he'll think I'm a downer—that I'm no fun and that I'm ruining our nice day. This is how my mother would react: She would tell me that I'm fine, that everything is happy. I think about this and force a smile, almost as if to please him. Pam had made me feel like I had the right to my emotions, and here I am with Patrick, who, I feel, only wants the happy parts of me. I don't think he will like it. I listen to the sound of the birds, of a lone frog in a nearby creek. *Just let it go*, I tell myself. I want to tell him all about her, how great she is, how hard she's fighting. How, in spite of our picnic and the sandwiches, I am sad. As I look at him, his face studying mine, something in his eyes, the way they hold my gaze, tells me that I can tell him.

51

Before Pam got sick, I might not have revealed to Patrick how devastated I was, how I was lost inside and felt great pain. I wouldn't have wanted him to see that part of me; I felt it was unattractive, or too intense. I would have continued having fun, telling jokes, laughing with him.

But grief is impossible not to share. Its burden is too heavy, and I am living under that weight. I can't pretend anymore to be okay. I keep trying to reach inside for comfort, but all I find is absence and pain. So I reach for Patrick.

I tell him about my panic attacks, a secret that no one knows other than my sisters and my parents. I explain the problems in my former marriage, why I worry it was all my fault. I talk to him about fears from my childhood, my obsession with perfection. I confess that I want, someday, to be a writer.

The days go by this way, with us meeting for gin and tonics at Clyde's in Georgetown, eggs Benedict at Martin's Tavern, and coffee at Kramers books in DuPont Circle. We go to movies and take walks in Rock Creek Park. We visit Mt. Vernon and spend the afternoon gazing out at the Potomac from the large wooden porch. We stop at a farm stand on the way home and buy cider and homemade jam.

Over time, Patrick begins to confess to me, too. He admits that his insecurity boils up at unexpected times, the lingering effects of a childhood spent feeling less than. He explains that his father was just a policeman, which no one else seemed to think was a very important job. Back then, his only peace was surfing—riding a wave, the water curling around him, inside "the little green room," as he calls it.

One day at lunch, we meet for pecan pie. Los Angeles might have lemon meringue, but nothing can compare to the Southern goodness of pecan. We are tucked in a booth at the Old Ebbitt Grill, a historic DC watering hole lined with dark wood paneling. It is dimly lit and it's cozy. We glance around and marvel at the dealmakers, the characters in showbusiness, the slick types, with flashy suits, big shoulders, wide lapels. I feel the same sense of comradery with Patrick as I felt with him six months ago, but now there is so much more. When I am with him I feel a sense of rootedness, as if time is tethered to the earth, so it isn't fleeting. As if the seconds expand to allow us to fit everything in, every story, every feeling, every word. This feels so sacred.

Then Patrick leans forward across the table, and he kisses me. It's the feeling of light in so much darkness. And I think to myself that love is the opposite of grief.

52

I look at my parents now and think about how far they have come. My mother's hair is pulled up into a French twist. She stands elegant in a Dior gown, perched alongside my father, dapper in his bespoke tuxedo. We are at the opening night of an exhibit at the National Gallery of Art. It is a classic Washington power event. Sponsored by Ford Motor Company and the British government, the Treasure Houses of Britain showcases art objects from more than two hundred country houses, representing five hundred years of history, in elaborate recreations of the rooms of grand homes in the English countryside. The champagne flows and power deals are brokered against a backdrop of paintings, furniture, tapestries, silver, and other precious items. The room is a sea of silk and taffeta gowns.

I spot Patrick entering through the main door and wave him over. Tonight is the night I introduce him to my parents. I am not sure what side of Patrick my parents will see. Will they see the son of a policeman who pulled himself up like they did, or will they see the telecommunications lawyer who has a big job in Washington?

"Mom, Dad, this is Patrick Doyle."

I watch as Patrick greets my parents. He smiles comfortably, undaunted. He stands straight, shoulders back, the scent of citrusy cologne exuding from him. I breathe a sigh of relief. I want Patrick to feel good around my parents. I want them to like each other.

I am the one who is nervous as I watch my father, looking squarely at Patrick, scanning his face. Is Dad trying to uncover something I might have missed? As if my life depends on a good sign from them. As if my own judgement these past months could be tossed aside in an instant by a disapproving grimace, a too-somber expression.

I listen as my father asks Patrick about people he knows in Washington and silently will Patrick to say names of people who are influential, so he can impress my father. I almost hold my breath. My father is familiar with a junior congressman on the foreign affairs committee whom Patrick is very close with. That's good. Not a real big deal, though. But Patrick knows Jack Valenti, president of the Motion Picture Association. *This* is a big deal. They've had lunch recently; not alone, with other people, but still. Valenti is a major power broker in this city and in Hollywood. I notice the corners of Dad's mouth move up, and this telegraphs to me that he is starting to enjoy himself. Then he smiles, nods his head, takes a sip of his cocktail, and I start to relax. He approves. I sigh with utter relief.

"Pam says you both have been having fun." My mother sounds cheerful. She surveys Patrick, as if she is admiring one of the sculptural objects on display in the museum.

The night, it seems, has been a success.

53

Over the next few weeks, my parents keep asking about Patrick. "How's his job?" my father wants to know. "Do his parents ever visit?" my mother inquires.

Patrick is routinely invited to dinner, and, when he's not busy with work or business travel or catching up with his own friends, he accepts. He and my father sit next to one another over drinks, like two pals sharing, inside the Beltway, stories and news of the latest satellite technology and communications.

One night while Patrick and my father are engaged in conversation, I slip away with my mother. She wants to show me a bag she's just bought, one she thinks I might like. We are standing in front of an immense closet in her dressing room. Mom holds up a brown, quilted-leather Chanel bag. "This is wonderful with your eyes,"

"Nothing completes an outfit like a good bag," I say happily, admiring the gold chain strap. I have been borrowing Mom's handbags lately, and getting my hair done regularly. I want to look my best. Patrick says he loves my hair short. He says it's "very Princess Diana." At the moment, my hair is cut in a pixie—poufy on top, requiring lots of hairspray. But I don't mind. I feel sophisticated. Even my colleagues at work have complimented me.

As I look in my mother's closet at the silks and the taffeta and the trimmed bouclé jackets, I am reminded of the endless amount of money my parents spent on my wedding—the champagne, the lily of the valley, the valet parking. Maybe I can make good on my lavish wedding, I think to myself. If the purpose of the extravaganza was to launch me into a life of happiness, then maybe by finally finding happiness, with Patrick, I can have what my parents wanted for me all along. I can find happiness *now*. What if all the toasts on the dance floor, the speech from the best man, my sister's words, my father at the mic in front of the Les Brown band, all the family and friends in the church, including the Reagans—what if they were really meant for now? What if there was just some sort of cosmic interference that placed my wedding to Robin in my life, where it never should have been? What if all that joy was meant for me and Patrick? I can't help but wonder, maybe I'm being given a second chance.

54

Two nights later, I listen to Patrick and my father talk about the big news of the day. We are in a booth at The Palm Restaurant. It is after work and the drinks are flowing and the crowd unwinds over steak and grilled potatoes. From international stories to domestic politics, there seems to be no end to the details. They discuss President Reagan's upcoming debate with former Vice President Mondale, the stir created by East German refugees seeking asylum in West Germany, and the Voice of America's latest broadcast.

I want to contribute to the conversation, but I can never interject fast enough. One moment I want to mention that a partner in our firm advised former Vice President Mondale. Another moment, the Motion Picture Association comes up, and I want to say I know about Jack Valenti fighting piracy. They are talking too fast for me to get a word in edgewise. The energy between Dad and Patrick is as if they are solving all the problems of the world.

Later in the conversation, my father and Patrick are in a heated discussion about the recent Soviet boycott of the Summer Olympics.

"They claimed it was about security." Patrick is earnest, as if he believes the Soviet excuse, but my father feels differently.

"Listen, Patrick, the Soviets wanted to make Ronnie look bad. That's what this was about."

"And retaliation because we boycotted the Olympics in '80?" Patrick surmises.

"Patrick, weren't you living in Virginia in 1980?" I ask out of context. And I am immediately cut off by my father, who looks at Patrick as if he is entirely missing the point.

"Hell, the Soviets had invaded Afghanistan. We had no choice but to boycott in '80." My father drains his glass of vodka, frustrated by Patrick.

"Was that the first time they invaded Afghanistan?" I wonder out loud.

"Charlie, I'm just saying there seems to be a history here, but I hear what you're saying," Patrick jumps in.

I am interested in the world, but there is just so much I don't know. I want so badly to be able to talk about the politics of Afghanistan and keep up with the conversation, but I was never encouraged to focus on newspaper headlines or current events and was I never self-motivated to do so. My whole life my mother shopped for blazers with me and my sisters. She wanted to make sure we had the right outfit for the right party when meeting the right people. I've trained my whole life to look the part, but not speak the part.

55

The day I decide that Patrick and I have a chance to be together, to have an actual future, we happen to be in the most unlikely place. We are at a Mobil station across from the Watergate on Virginia Avenue. It is night. I am in the passenger side of his car and watch him walk into the gas station to pay for fuel. There is nothing remarkable about this moment. There are a few car headlights in the distance. Patrick stops for a moment, checks his wallet. He looks down, his face illuminated by the glare of the fluorescent lights above. I notice how handsome he looks in his dark suit and tie. But what I mostly notice is how he is so in charge: the way he holds himself, the way he purposely walks toward the register to pay—he's just so unafraid of being in the world.

Later that night, after he drops me off at my apartment, I daydream about the life we might have. Three kids. Christmas carols during the holidays; summer; playing tennis in tennis whites; our daughter, velvet hat and boots, winning first place at horse shows. I'll pack ham sandwiches and thermoses of lemonade. We will all pile into our station wagon and stop at Will Wright's on the way home for ice cream.

And then I realize that my name would be Mrs. Patrick Doyle. I envision my new monogram: the "P" for Pam, the "D" for Doyle, two large red letters on cream cardstock in the most elegant Baskerville script letters. I've always loved that font.

"Two boxes of five hundred," I would tell the woman at the stationery store.

"Of course, Mrs. Doyle," she would respond. "Happy to help you with that today."

Pam Doyle. There is a nice ring to it, a safety, the idea that I am exactly where I am supposed to be.

So, two hours later I am surprised when I feel the familiar warning signs of a panic attack coming on. Standing in front of the mirror in my bathroom, I take off my makeup. Suddenly I feel a tingling. My chest tightens. My heart begins to pound. Blood rushes to my ears. Sweat beads on my upper lip. I can't breathe. A train barreling down the tracks, impossible to stop. No stopping. "In breath, slooowww, out breath, slowww. Relax..." I tell myself. I look in the mirror, I look at my hair—does this hair belong to me? My gaze looks different. I don't know what it is. My eyes are not mine. I don't recognize myself. I don't know who this is—this person staring back at me. I don't know who I am. I am back in California, inside our house, running into our dining room. I am little. I take cover under the antique, dark wood chair with the calming floral upholstery. I scrunch up tightly. Then I find safety. This is where I lose my fear.

56

The next day it is as if the panic attack never happened. Patrick and I are strolling through Rock Creek Park under a canopy of maple and hickory trees with red and gold leaves. We step over boulders and pieces of branches on the trail. Though we are only a few miles from the White House, this is a peaceful refuge. Everything about this moment is perfect. It's Saturday. Patrick looks relaxed, a calm expression on his face. I know he feels as good as I do. I watch him navigate a large rock, then plop down on top of it. He pats the flat grey surface next to him, indicating I join him. I climb onto the rock and take my seat.

There are more such moments where we don't feel the need to talk. I close my eyes, listen to the gurgling of the creek, the chirping of migratory birds. I feel warm sunlight on my face. I open my eyes a few moments later and see that Patrick is staring at my sweater. I follow his gaze down and spot a tiny moth hole in the weave, near the neck. His expression has shifted into a slight frown; he looks as if he's just found a flaw in our glossy postcard of a day. This surprises me and I'm not quite sure what to do. It's just a hole in my sweater. But I can tell that this has dampened his mood. I get nervous at first, then antsy very quickly. I wish I could make the moment good again. I explain that I just grabbed the sweater and didn't notice. I think about my mother, how she'd never let me be caught dead with a moth hole.

But why do I have to explain? We're in the country, not at a black-tie event. I watch Patrick, hoping that his expression will shift back to peaceful. But he seems slightly tense.

"You'll get it fixed," he says with an admonishing smile as he reaches up and pulls my shirt collar over the hole so it's out of view.

I hesitate. There is something unfamiliar about him doing this… it feels strange. But I think Patrick is comfortable being himself. He's being honest. That's a good thing. He thinks I should fix the hole in my sweater. He's looking out for me. I watch the creek below, water *whooshing* over rocks. I breathe in slowly. What if this is the part of him I've yet to experience?

57

Patrick redeems himself the following day—or, rather, there is no tense look on his face. He is so caring as he hands me a glass of wine. We are at a fundraiser hosted by the Young Republicans organization. A downtown restaurant is filled with eager, fresh-faced twenty- and thirty-year-olds, young men in suits, young women in tailored dresses, Reagan/Bush '84 posters, tables set up to register young future GOPs, and campaign lapel buttons in glass bowls for the cost of a few dollars. The presidential election is next month and the excitement is palpable.

President Reagan has just performed spectacularly in his second debate with Walter Mondale, and his poll numbers have jumped. Everyone is talking about it tonight. Especially the part of the debate when President Reagan brought the house down by exclaiming, when asked about his age as the oldest president in history, "I will not make age an issue of this campaign. I am not going to exploit, for political purposes, my opponent's youth and inexperience."

"You look great, sweetie." Patrick admires my red wool skirt and the gold chain of my mother's Chanel handbag over my shoulder. He always wants me to look my best and I know I've succeeded in pleasing him tonight.

"I want you to meet someone." Patrick guides me through the crowd. "The guy's real important to us. Lead counsel on the House telecommunications committee. Big fan of Ron Dog."

I nod, *Got it*. This means I will pay attention, make a good impression; maybe I can help Patrick by being extra engaging. This makes me feel useful, important even.

Patrick introduces me to Tom and Amy. She wears glasses, has blonde hair, and is very pregnant. Tom is preppy in a plaid bow tie, a "Reagan/Bush '84" button pinned to his lapel. I make a big effort when I greet them. We talk about President Reagan's performance in the debates.

"Wasn't he amazing?" I say, looking at Tom and Amy, watching for their reaction, hoping they like me.

Tom jumps in enthusiastically. "Ronald Reagan's my hero."

"Pam's dad is Charlie Wick," Patrick announces.

I am a tad uncomfortable as he says this, hoping that memories in DC are as short as they are in Hollywood. To my relief, Amy and Tom don't register a negative reaction. "Your dad has done a great job. Incredible," Tom says enthusiastically. My father's scandal is no longer the topic of conversation. The awful, gut-wrenching sensation of the past few months, the front-page stories, the Senate hearings, witnessing my parents suffer. It has finally subsided.

"Your dad has put the USIA back on the map. The Soviets don't know what hit 'em." Tom looks at me as if I had something to do with this. It's funny. As if I am the one who's influential. Doesn't he see that I haven't done anything? I am just a stand-in, a placeholder for my father's accomplishments.

But for Patrick, everything is okay. More than okay.

Patrick tells Tom and Amy that my father co-chaired Reagan's presidential inaugural four years ago.

"Sure." Tom smiles at me with seemingly new respect. "Your dad co-chaired with Bob Gray. What a team. We went to one of the galas."

Patrick adds, "And Pam's mother Mary Jane is best friends with *the* Nancy."

Tom and Amy are a little awed by me, as if *I'm* something special. As if Tom is no longer searching for my father. That by association, *I'm* accomplished and interesting. I'm not just a stand-in. Because I'm a firsthand witness to my father's greatness, and, as his daughter, I am in the inner sanctum.

I want to say something else to turn the spotlight on Amy and Tom. I could ask her about her pregnancy or mention Tom's distinctive bow tie—Senator Pat Moynihan wears one, too; he must know this. But Patrick won't let the topic go.

Tom and Amy seem amazed by *me*. But Patrick looks the most pleased. I have done well for us.

58

In the weeks that follow, I have the strangest sense of feeling less and less like myself and more and more like "the person related to Charles Wick." It is unsettling and leaves me feeling like a dry, parched desert. Me. As though I am not enough. As though I am actually a deficit, a nagging reminder of the fact that I am not the real person of interest, that I am not my father.

Everywhere I go with Patrick, I feel as if I'm on parade. A dinner at the National Press Club. A gala held at the Hirshhorn Museum. A fundraising luncheon at the Ritz-Carlton. I am so aware that I am "Charlie Wick's daughter."

At the Safeway in Georgetown, we bump into an important lobbyist. He's carrying a can of kidney beans in his shopping basket. "Did you know Pam's mother and Nancy ran the chili booth at their grade-school fair?" Patrick finds a way to weave into the conversation some story about me, calculated to impress, as if it were logical. Every time.

I know Patrick appreciates me for *me*. He appreciates my sense of humor, my insight into things, my warmth. But I also feel his drive to be important, to be at the center of power. And dating Charlie Wick's daughter puts him there.

But why am I worrying about this? What Patrick is saying is true. He's telling people things that are true. So I start to relax and decide not to make all this such a big deal. Maybe he's proud of me, maybe it's as simple as that.

59

The last rays of daylight filter into my parents' kitchen through the window.

I watch as my mother carefully slices a tomato, her capable hand guiding the knife through the skin. She is focused, and yet she seems vulnerable somehow.

She places the slices onto a colorful china plate. She is making hamburgers tonight.

Mom looks down at the tomatoes, a strand of hair loose from her well-coiffed bun. It occurs to me that she is not the same as she was before my parents moved to Washington. I can see it in her face. Sometimes I look at her and I notice new lines on her forehead. I think that Washington put these lines on her face. There is a tightness to her mouth that wasn't there before. And it pulls her answers closer in to her—she measures every word she says. She has a wall around her that politics has built.

Now she takes a package of ground meat from the refrigerator and checks the date.

I don't know if this is the right moment to have a frank discussion with her, but I ask the question that has been on my mind anyway. "You do like Patrick, right?"

My mother has an uncanny way of seeing to the heart of people, of looking past all the things they layer on outside to hide who they really are. If anyone knows what Patrick's intentions are, it will be my mother.

She takes a moment, her hands under the cold water. Then she turns to me, a look of calm.

"It doesn't matter what I think. You have to do what's right for you, honey."

But this isn't an answer. And it annoys me. When she doesn't want to say how she really feels, this is the kind of answer she gives. My mother stands behind her Midwestern inscrutability. She holds her truth close to her. I've seen her do it with people we know. They walk away satisfied, having no idea that they don't have an answer. And now she's doing it with me.

60

I imagine turning out like my mother, having her life. I'd always assumed I'd have her life. I'd be elegant in Dior and Chanel evening gowns. I'd manage the house and children, give dinner parties to influential people, and make my husband look good. I'd support causes, I'd serve on boards like Ford's Theatre, and I'd spearhead efforts to get speed bumps on our home's Hollywood celebrity street in Los Angeles. Of course, my husband and I would want safety for the residents in our neighborhood.

Perhaps being a wife in Washington is a supporting role. Still, it comes with its own kind of power. Both my father and President Reagan consider their wives their closest advisors, and behind closed doors I often hear my mother telling my father, "Charles, look, you're not doing yourself any favors." She often sees the best course of action before he does, and he usually takes her suggestions. Mrs. R trumps any cabinet member, congressman, or senator. President Reagan turns to her and trusts her implicitly.

At the height of our family's public scandal, Dad was resistant to Len's idea to systematically apologize to those he had taped. He thought it could backfire. My mother felt otherwise. "Charles, you can't possibly know how this works. Listen to Len." I watched my dad quietly take in her words. "Mary Jane, you're right," he conceded. My father tends to be trusting—like a golden retriever—but my mother is shrewd, slow to trust others, and hard to read—like a Siamese cat.

This is the kind of future I imagine I will have with Patrick, wielding behind-the-scenes power. I daydream about this on a crisp, fall Sunday morning. Patrick makes coffee in my small galley kitchen. I am curled up on my sofa, flipping through *Town & Country* magazine. It is exciting. I haven't felt this way in so long. I imagine what my life can be. Or rather, our life. Me and Patrick. We will live in a big house like the ones in the magazine, invite friends to dinner, seat them at our dining table—forks, spoons, and knives in proper order, Mozart filling the air from our stereo, manicured lawns extending out to intricately trimmed hedges and red maple and birch trees. As Patrick walks in carrying two cups of coffee, he takes a seat next to me on the sofa. I enthusiastically show him the magazine.

"Which do you like, hedges or gates for privacy?"

He glances at the glossy spread. I watch him, sipping his coffee in his terry robe. He looks peaceful, a face only I get to see. Usually he is serious and harried, rushing around, late for an appointment or a dinner. I know we both want this, a life together. I glance around my apartment, thinking how it has been a stepping stone to a better future.

Then we begin to have a conversation I can only describe as a fantasy. It's the kind of conversation that I've always wanted. The prelude to a secure life. We discuss the type of house we would live in. Patrick is a fan of English Tudor. I prefer clapboard, a large veranda.

"You can learn to garden," he says with enthusiasm.

I imagine a canvas apron with pockets for garden tools—me potting colorful flowers. Not only will I garden, I can learn to bake in our big kitchen, I tell myself. Apple pies in fall, peach in summer. A sweetness overtakes me as my thoughts swirl through my head. Building a life with Patrick is a dream.

"I'll garden and bake on weekends, but Monday through Friday it'll be all business. We'll each go to our offices. I'll move my way up to an associate in our firm, or maybe I'll work at a museum and take advantage of my art history degree."

Patrick gives me a funny look.

"Granted, it'll be hectic. I'll get dressed in the morning, grab my briefcase, run out the door. 'See you at seven,' I'll say."

"Is that how you think it will be?" snaps Patrick. His mood has changed.

The joy of my scenario seeps out of me. Doesn't he share my vision?

"Wha...what did you have in mind?" I finally ask after a few moments of just staring at him. Maybe my dreams of a house are too grand. Maybe he thinks I'm entitled or pretentious. Maybe he just hates apple pie. But I'm flexible. I can live in a small house. I can learn to bake cherry instead of apple.

There is nothing he can say to make the fantasy life disappear. I will adapt to whatever he has in mind.

"When you are married to me, you're not going to work."

He looks back down at the magazine, seemingly unaware of his words. As if he casually *told* me what I will be doing. How can he contentedly sip his coffee? What about *my* opinion? *My* feelings? How can he tell me what I'll be doing, as if I have no say in my own life? I feel a rise of annoyance. My face becomes flushed. I glance around my living room and my garden view. The fall tree dropping its leaves— it's just empty and sad. But I don't say anything because I don't know what to say.

61

The next day at the office I can't stop thinking about Patrick. I can't keep my mind on my job. Instead, I continually replay the previous day's scene in my head—being in my apartment, the cozy Sunday morning, fresh coffee, the glossy magazine photos. I can't get over what he said, how his mood shifted. It's the *way* he said the thing about me not working. It was like an order—he told me, he didn't ask, and yet he had no idea he had done this.

I have forty-five minutes before my next meeting so I decide to call my mom. She is razor sharp about people.

"What do you think he meant?" I ask after telling her what Patrick said about our future.

By the time she makes an assessment, it's as if she's looked at the person through a prism and come out with the same conclusion from every angle.

"Well...." My mother's voice trails off.

She sounds evasive at the other end of the line. I can tell she's preoccupied, the way she "uh huhs" and "mm-mmms" as if she's only partially listening to me. Her mind is somewhere else. I glance at unopened files on my desk; I have a lot to do. But all I can focus on is the fact that my mother is worried. Maybe it's about something with my father, maybe she's sneaking a cigarette before he gets home. Maybe she doesn't want to tell me what she really thinks.

The last time I asked her opinion of Patrick, she shrugged it off and simply said, "It's your life." This time I am hoping to get more out of her, to understand how she really feels.

Finally, my mother comes around and says, "Do you find him a bit controlling?" The way she says it is offhanded, the same way she'd ask if I'd like another helping of dessert, as if I shouldn't read too much into her question, as if there is no one right answer.

I get up to make sure my office door is shut, not wishing my conversation to be overheard by someone walking down the office hallway. *Is Patrick controlling?* I wonder as I sit back down at my desk. I don't think so; he loves me.

If my mother felt this way, why has she never said anything? Instead, she lent me her Chanel bag for parties and cheered me on as I happily waltzed out the door.

"Mom, so what do mean? What do you notice?"

I just want a straight answer. But she doesn't give one. Instead of confronting, my mother prefers "planting the seed" in my mind. She dangles out her idea in the form of a question so I will take it and absorb it. "Don't you like the navy instead of the beige?" This way she can make me feel as if I have made my own decision. And I always make my decision, which is really *her* decision.

However, the seed has been planted and she won't offer any more.

Mom says she has to hang up because my father is coming home soon and they're going to a reception at the State Department.

Before she gets off the phone, she has one final thing to say. "You don't need to rush into anything." This stops me. A red sign. A warning. In this one sentence, it's as if she's finally come out and said how she feels.

* * *

"WHAT DO YOU THINK?" CINDY ASKS ME. I am at home, sprawled out on my sofa, talking to my sister over the phone. The conversation is starting to sound exactly like the one I had earlier with my mother.

I hesitate. I realize I always think what everyone else thinks. And now that my mother might not agree with my thinking, I don't know *what* to think. Then I say, "Patrick is great," because I do think that about him, in spite of what my mother says. But then again I'm not so sure.

"There must be things..." Cindy digs.

"Not really."

I don't want to tell my sister. Yet at the same time I do. I'm not sure if I want to defend Patrick or get to the truth.

I feel a bolt of courage so I start to let it out. I tell Cindy about Rock Creek Park, the day Patrick and I were in the warm sun, relaxing, and about how good it felt until he discovered the tiny moth hole in my sweater. How that changed everything. As if the day was no longer drenched in sunshine.

"All my sweaters have moth holes; what's wrong with that?" Cindy says.

But there are so many good things. I tell my sister how he seems so proud to be with me. "He's proud I'm Charles Wick's daughter. He thinks Dad is amazing. Nothing wrong with that," I conclude.

Then I tell Cindy how I helped Patrick with Tom at the young Republican event and how good that felt.

"Young Republican?" She starts to laugh.

"It's not funny. They work hard," I say, thinking about the packed cocktail party.

My sisters and my brothers are not Republicans. They are Democrats and anti-Republicans, in fact, in spite of the Reagans being family friends. They don't live in the cocoon that is Washington and instead are living their own lives with people who think differently and who question everything around them. The rest of us live in the Reagan bubble.

"If Mom thinks he's controlling, you must have told her something else."

Then I finally describe what Patrick said about my not working when I'm married to him. The *way* he told me.

But what I don't tell Cindy, and I haven't told my mother, is what I've buried deep inside. Patrick is quick to erupt in anger and is unpredictable. He is "Jekyll and Hyde," in his own words. He says he can't help being this way. Once, when I talked to a stranger in Rock Creek Park, he angrily accused me of flirting. When I explained why I thought Republicans should consider voting in favor of the ERA, he was fuming. When I bought Muenster cheese instead of Swiss, it ruined our night. So when he said that I wouldn't be working when I was married to him, it wasn't so much his *words* as the *anger* I sensed from him. It was as if who he really is—the full person—was laid bare in front of me.

I don't even need to hear my sister's words. My answer has come to me unbidden. It is mildly terrifying, but I feel a strange sense of release.

62

The next day, as if on autopilot, I do something I never counted on. I break up with Patrick. The event is less emotional than I would have anticipated. He is over for dinner. We are at my small dining table, finishing our take-out chicken and salads. I watch him talking about his day. He enthusiastically motions with his hands, politely trying not to talk with food in his mouth. "I was good in the meeting, it wasn't easy, these guys were so off...." I nod, listening. Then, suddenly, the words spill out of me: "I can't feel safe with you and I don't want to spend my life this way." I hear the hum of my refrigerator. My stomach is in a knot. I can't believe I did this.

He puts his fork down. His face loses all expression. He seems shocked. He puts his head down for a moment. Then he looks back up at me, and it's sad. He pleads with me, saying he'll change. "This isn't fair; I need you, sweetie."

But inside of me something has turned cold. I say no. Any warmth I felt, any possibility, has been snuffed out. I know I'll cry over him later, but right now all I feel is numb. It's not even courage, as I think about it—it's that I get this reprieve from feeling anything so it allows me to make the right decision.

63

I step out of bed the next morning and the floor feels cold. I am in a stupor. I am the aftermath of a storm. Quiet and still. An empty Kleenex box and discarded tissues are the only evidence of my torrential night. My throat is scratchy from crying so hard. I replay my conversation with Patrick. Done. Over. No more. But after he left, being alone in my apartment feels so sad, so hopeless. A sob finds its way up and out of me. Then another. I walk down my small hallway, still in my pajamas, to the bathroom and pour cold water onto my face. It feels like a slap. I need to leave for work.

Later, in a staff meeting, I fight back tears. I stare down at my legal pad to read something. Then I look around at my colleagues and wonder who is happy and who is not. I watch as Bob gestures with his hands, his wedding ring catching the light. He is talking about a bill in Congress. Anne, at the head of the table, interjects a point. A lawyer across from her makes another point. Some wear wedding rings, some sip coffee, some take notes. Have they ever felt lost? Utterly lost? I look at a vase of sunflowers on the conference table. So cheery, as if it's mocking me. I imagine a bright-orange pumpkin on my colleague's front porch where they will go home and drink apple cider. This is what I want. To feel safe. And happy.

After work one day I go to my parents' house. "There is no more Patrick," I tell my mother when she asks what is new. She looks at me and she says she's sorry, but I know she is relieved. I can tell because she seems sad for an instant, then her eyes widen and she cheerfully asks if I want to join my parents at The Jockey Club for dinner. "You love their crab cakes. Bill and Sofia Casey will be there," she says, as if to move my life along. But my life won't move. It tipped over. I'm in a ditch. I am stuck. In a kind of darkness.

I know that I am sad about the breakup. But there is also something else going on, something I don't quite know how to explain. It's as if everything is coming on at once. Now when I feel the tears staring to appear, I don't know whether it's about Patrick, Pam getting sick, my father's scandal, or Robin—or all of it together. This year has been a series of giant, incomprehensible fails (though Pam's sickness is in a category all its own). The weight of it all. It's bewildering.

I try to carry on. I wipe my eyes and use some Visine. I put on a good front at work, but when I am alone, I think about how I no longer know good from bad, truth from lies. I no longer know who or what to believe.

All my life I have been taught to do the right thing. "Be a good girl; you will have a happy life" was what my parents promised me time and time again. Go to the right school. Marry the right man. Socialize with the right people. And I did all of those things. And where did it get me? Lonely in a marriage that was too traditional for me, working at a job I never would have chosen myself.

The right thing? Haven't I tried my whole life to do "the right thing"? Haven't I tried so hard to be just like my mother and father? Dad tried so hard to do the right thing. But one mistake and his life was taken out from under him.

And what about Pam? Didn't she always try to do the right thing? Pam with her ERA mug; Pam who was always fighting for the rights of women. What good is it trying to change the world if you become terminally ill before you're even fifty?

And then there was Robin. He did the right things. He went to Yale, got his MBA, worked his way up the corporate banking ladder, and married a girl his parents liked. But I wasn't enough for him.

And now, it's as if I can't count on life. It's as if my north has become my south. Some magnetic field has switched my cardinal points and I don't recognize where I am. My whole life I've been taught where north is, to go toward that, and now it's not there anymore. Everything's flipped. The rules I grew up with have changed. Everything I trusted has dissolved.

64

"I'm worried about you. You don't return my calls. I've left messages. Mom's worried about you."

Cindy is on the other line. The tone of her voice is warm. It's a voice I know so well; in her words I feel the safety of our childhood. "Are you okay?"

It is her kindness that makes me start to cry, the reminder that I am not completely alone. For the past few days, I haven't reached out to my family. No one knows where I am. It hasn't occurred to me. I've been in bed. I called in sick to work. I didn't want to walk by Pam's office, hear my parents' voice—it's all just too much.

"Pam...you're going to get through this." Cindy is practically pleading with me.

"That's what mom always says. But it's never true. And this time it is not going to be okay."

"You just need to be taken care of for a little while. You need to rest. Why don't you let me take care of you? Come to New York."

Speaking to her, I feel a tiny sliver of hope. Cindy has always known how to be there for me. When we were little, she would sit across from me for as long as it took for me to tell her what was wrong whenever I was upset. She made me soup when I was sick. It's not so much the taste I remember, but the image of her, dragging a chair to the kitchen counter, standing on top of it, and fumbling with the can opener to pry open the Campbell's soup. She never got it hot enough, but it still tasted good.

65

Cindy throws her arms around me and I am engulfed by her tall frame; she smells like soap and Charlie perfume. Her peasant blouse, faded jeans, messy ponytail—she is my home. Everything inside me sort of melts into a calm. I take a big breath, and notice a carved pumpkin at her entryway. Cindy leads me into her bedroom and motions to her messy bed, piled with pillows.

"I'm bringing you lunch on a tray."

She hands me a pair of sweats and a T-shirt.

"Get cozy."

I look back at my sister, the concern apparent on her face. Sometimes we've joked that we share the same heart. In this moment, it feels as if I am relaxing into the rhythm of *our* heart. Slowing down, settling back into myself.

We spend the afternoon talking. I tell her about Washington. About everything. I am propped up on pillows; she is sitting next to me, listening.

"It must have been so hard, being there, all alone."

Soon after, I fall asleep.

It is dusk when I awaken. I have a slight headache. At the same time I am relieved. I feel as if some sadness has been lessened and I feel lighter. I look out across the bedroom through my sister's windows, the silhouette of water towers on old brick buildings. The sky is blue and pinkish.

"Okay, we're going to my boss's for drinks," she says.

Cindy is a survivor. "Good cry, get it out." That's her motto. She is like our mother. I, on the other hand, can linger interminably in darkness. Like our father. My sister has a way of pulling me back into the world. I am grateful, even if a bit shaky and unsure.

I step out of bed. Cindy looks me over; I know what she's thinking. I'm too thin. Her eyebrows knit together as she scrutinizes my loafers and my khaki pants, which I threw onto a chair. I know she thinks my clothes are too preppy, too formal.

"You bring anything more casual?"

"I am not casual. Washington, DC, is not casual," I tell her.

Everything there is formal and consequential, and everything is serious: attorneys, hydroelectric power, political scandals, press conferences. So I didn't bring anything casual because I wouldn't know how or when to wear it.

"I'll lend you something."

Cindy apparently wants to burn my khakis. She tosses them in her trash and picks out a knit crochet dress, very boho. I'd never buy this dress. But I throw it over my head, and, although large on me, it gently drapes over my hips.

"See? You look better already." Cindy admires me.

* * *

THROUGH THE CAB WINDOW, MANHATTAN IS LIT UP like one of my mother's crystal-encrusted Judith Leiber handbags. It literally sparkles against the autumn night sky and I feel a slight thrill as I gaze out at the explosion of color.

We arrive at her boss's building, made of curved steel and smoked glass, and he is perched at his open doorway, grinning. George is not classically handsome, but he is well-proportioned and dressed unlike anyone in Washington: jeans, a Barry Kieselstein-Cord belt with a giant silver buckle, and black snakeskin boots.

"It's nice to meet you." His voice is gravelly and his Greek accent almost musical.

"My sister Pam," Cindy introduces us.

"Lovely sister." George is flirting with me.

I find him sexy. He is hip and his laugh, genuine. He smells like musk, and I am surprised by my reaction to him because I'm feeling a sliver of excitement. He's unlike anything I've known. No shirt and tie, no pressed khakis.

Now George looks at me like he's seeing something I have no idea is there. He kind of squints as he studies me, as if another Pam comes into focus. Do I have a twin sister who is sexy and filled with possibility?

He takes my hand and leads me to his ultramodern kitchen, where he has uncorked a bottle of expensive champagne. Cindy follows, explaining to him how depressed I am, as though she expects him to fix me. Or like they have taken in a stray and he must feed me.

"You must try my beluga caviar—gives you strength," George offers.

Moments later we sit drinking champagne and eating caviar, overlooking the East River, bold skyscrapers, and the neon Pepsi sign blinking red in the distance.

The champagne flushes my headache away, and I feel happy, even. Cindy and George describe the poster they've designed for the movie *Flashdance*. George owns a film marketing company and Paramount is their big client. The star, Jennifer Beals, sits on a threadbare Persian rug, glancing up at the camera, looking utterly cool. George holds the poster up. I can tell he's really proud of their work.

"She's in heels, her sweatshirt top over one shoulder, like a dancer," he explains.

"We had to submit, like, eight ideas to Paramount," Cindy adds.

George asks me if I like the poster. I respond with a resounding thumbs up. I point to the red high heels Beals is wearing and tell them how I think that is such a good touch, the color—it's unexpected. George listens to me as if he actually cares. I feel so at ease; he genuinely seems to be enjoying my company.

My broken life feels a million miles away and I begin to relax more, not just a loosening of my neck and shoulders, but on a deep, cellular level, as if my life is slowly rewinding itself and making room for some kind of newer, better version.

66

My sister's neighborhood, Columbus Avenue, is a mix of bars and restaurants, delis, dry cleaners, and second-hand clothing boutiques. Cindy and I dodge piled-up trash, listen to a street quartet playing Vivaldi, and watch an artist sketch portraits for five dollars. The air is cool off the Hudson. I feel as if I snuck out to another life.

"You remember Robbie? We're meeting him for coffee. We need to cheer him up; he's going through a bad time."

Robbie Browne is my sister's former boyfriend. They went out for several months, but the sex was almost nonexistent. "He just wasn't interested." Cindy told me that Robbie began to realize he was gay. And as my sister always knows what to do, she said that she was happy for him, and she got to work trying to find him a boyfriend. Robbie eventually came out publicly and has marched in every gay parade since.

Now he sits across from us in a booth at a coffee shop. With a strong jawline, Princeton-grad preppiness, and his wrinkled Oxford shirt, Robbie looks like he has everything going for him. He's not the kind of person one would look at and say, "It's obvious that tragedy has struck him." But he has lost two friends and he is devastated.

"They were sick, then gone." He looks off.

Cindy and I don't know what to say. Robbie's eyes are swollen with tears.

"They have to find a cure," my sister says, taking his hand.

Robbie doesn't seem hopeful. I can't imagine losing *two* friends. I can't imagine anything worse than Pam getting sick. How does it feel to wonder which of your friends might be sick next? Or if you yourself will be? He must feel helpless. It occurs to me that no one in Washington talks enough about what is happening to all these young men. As I watch Robbie, life suddenly feels bleak. Some kids laugh loudly at the counter, an older couple shuffle by, the man holding the woman's arm. Though we try to do the right thing, there is no guarantee. And now, this person who has just been living his life finds it shattering around him. My fun from last night dissolves and leaves me empty.

We hug Robbie goodbye on the busy sidewalk. Cindy wipes a tear from her eye.

Then, surprisingly, he stops us. He takes in a huge breath and pushes all his air out. He starts to smile. It's almost like he willed himself to do this.

"You coming tonight? It's going to be a blast!"

Now he looks at us, excited. He tells us that he and his friends are marching in the Halloween parade. Cindy can't go. She has a photo shoot.

"Pam, please? Come for drinks?" He looks right at me. "Patti's coming."

I think of seeing Patti Reagan again; I haven't seen her since Christmas. It would be nice—Patti is practically family. And in this moment I'd do anything to cheer Robbie up. So I tell him yes.

* * *

JEZEBEL IS MY SISTER'S FAVORITE THRIFT STORE, and she is intent on a makeover for me. I don't want to remind her again that secondhand jeans and crochet dresses are unwearable in Washington. But for now, what difference does it make? I can pretend this is my life. I have almost a week here; I'm finally using my piled-up vacation days.

Cindy ushers me into a musty 1930s building with concrete floors and exposed brick walls. My sister has changed gears and now she is back to taking care of me. "We'll find you something great."

Once inside, the scent of mothballs and dust fills the air. All around me are racks of "tenderly loved" items—leather jackets, flannel shirts, silk dresses, trench coats, button-down white shirts, a few silk bomber jackets, art deco jewelry. I feel as if I'm in the wardrobe department for a high school play or a Broadway show. I'm in a make-believe world where there is no sorrow, no stress, and no regrets.

Cindy tosses another pair of jeans into my dressing room. I wriggle into them as I hear her chatter with a saleswoman.

"She needs a whole new wardrobe. No more men's clothing."

Slowly I start to feel better. It feels so good to allow Cindy to lead me into what she wants for me. It is like a slow-motion, long-overdue rebellion. I realize I don't think I've ever had one. I never stayed out late, or snuck alcohol or cigarettes, or tried pot. Well, one time at Berkeley, I ate marijuana lasagna laced with angel dust, but I had no idea. It terrified me; I was high for a week. I always felt so safe doing what I thought I was supposed to do. I finally button up the very tight Levi's jeans and walk out of the dressing room. Cindy gasps.

"Oh, my God, you're sexy."

I look at my reflection in the mirror; she tosses a purple denim jacket over my shoulders. Part Annie Hall, part biker girl. I actually have hips, and a waist! *I look cool*, I think. It's kind of like a rugged Cinderella moment. My sense of excitement revs from zero to sixty. I run my hands down my hips, and wonder to myself, *Could I go to the Congressional wives luncheon wearing this?* Nope. Then it occurs to me: Is this who I really am? Have I been someone else all these years? Was I just being who I thought I was supposed to be? Am I really *this*? Maybe I could have a creative job like Cindy? Or a job in publishing? Or advertising or copywriting? Or experiment with different kinds of jobs? Maybe I'm now being Cindy's idea of a woman, and not my idea of a woman. But what *is* my idea of a woman, really?

I get a tugging sensation, and the words "What are you doing? Get back to your life" play in my head. The "adult" me, with twelve place settings of china, a recent breakup, and a pending divorce, says, "Return to the dressing room, change into your men's clothes, go back to Cindy's apartment, fish your khakis out of her trash, and take the train back to Washington where you must shed this frivolous new life and put back on your old one." It is the oddest feeling, as if I am being disloyal to my established self, the one created by my parents. But this feeling lasts for only a moment; then I look back in the mirror.

67

Walking into Robbie's apartment, I am hit by a raucous, fun scene. A dozen of his vibrant gay friends are in silk, chiffon, and taffeta; there are piles of skirts, and a few fur coats are lying around. Donna Summer's "She Works Hard for the Money" blasts from the stereo. The guys are getting ready for the Halloween parade, and going in costume—or, more accurately, drag. Robbie, in a brightly colored kaftan, welcomes me by putting a drink in my hand. I honestly can't believe that he is able to be so cheerful after seeing him earlier today. I spot Patti Reagan, who rushes over and greets me warmly. Patti and Robbie are longtime friends.

The three of us stand together—Robbie, his bold red lipstick adding a touch of glamour to his face; Patti in her tank top and ripped jeans, sipping her wine spritzer; and me, nearly divorced. It's as though we have fallen down the rabbit hole of rules, landing in an Alice-in-Wonderland world. Everything is upside down. I should be home with my husband and children, tucking our little ones into bed. Patti should be at the White House with a proper boyfriend, dining over candlelight with her parents and some ambassador and his wife. And Robbie should be with his adoring wife at their country club, enjoying grilled fish and roasted fingerling potatoes. But instead, we are here. Each of us in our own way, not where we are *supposed* to be. And rather than upset me, I find a sense of possibility. I feel a tingling along the back of my neck, which both scares me and invigorates me.

"Ladies, assist with makeup?" Robbie motions to beauty supplies on the coffee table.

Patti and I look at each other. Why not?

So, I reach for some makeup brushes. I've never smoothed base makeup over beard stubble. And I can't ask Patti—she's across the room, already laughing with one of Robbie's friends who's modeling a gown.

A half hour later, I feel like a full-fledged makeup artist.

"More mascara?" I say, holding up the wand to a wavy-haired man wearing a lime green minidress and neon-pink tights.

"Just a tad," he instructs me.

Tom, effusive and chubby, is in his third year of med school at Columbia. He has round eyes. My mother would think he's such a catch, and she might not even care that he's gay.

"Do *not* rub your eyes; it'll look like you got into a fight," I instruct him.

I'm sort of jealous of Tom's eyelashes—they're so long and thick.

Robbie walks up to me, in a skirt, his muscular calves peeking out under the taffeta.

"Is it me? What d'you think?"

A big grin on his face, he's actually serious, in a sort of parallel-universe way, as if he might be banished from newspaper fashion pages if he doesn't get this right.

"Why not try those silk palazzo pants?" I tell him, playing along, as I motion to the colorful Pucci wide-leg pants tossed onto the sofa.

"Really? You think?"

I imagine Robbie strutting down the runway at New York Fashion Week, a highly paid model, his strong, hairy legs mystifying Anna Wintour, who takes notes from her front row seat.

"*These* Pucci pants!" I grab them. "Robbie, they're *you*."

I hand them to him; he gives them a once-over, tilting his head side to side.

Then he pulls off his skirt, strips down to his undies, and wriggles into the delicate fabric of the pants.

"Striking!" Robbie twirls, modeling the Pucci pants, which are way above his ankles.

"So Palm Beach, so C.Z. Guest," he muses excitedly.

"Yes, you, poolside, lounging, long cigarette in one hand." I nod.

He is a vision with his blonde hair and peachy skin.

"I just realized, you're a summer. These Pucci pastel colors are perfect!"

"Makeup refresh!" Robbie motions to his cheeks.

I reach for the brushes and begin to apply pink blush to his face.

The music blares; there's chatter, laughter, excitement. This must be what New York Fashion Week is like. Only, instead of reed-thin models, these are hulking, deep-voiced divas.

"Too bad—you'd love my Fendi pumps, but they're not here and you'd never fit into a seven," I tell Robbie.

"Fendi? No, no. Jimmy Choo! Givenchy!"

"Darling, *désolé, nous n'en avons pas*," I say in my best French.

An hour later, we are all trotting down Central Park West under a full moon on a perfect, fall New York night. The guys are primped, coiffed, dazzlingly dressed, as the rustling skirts, silky dresses, and designer purses fill the sidewalk. I think, in the face of sadness and despair, these men just roll with it. In spite of all that Robbie is going through—and, no doubt, what many of his friends are as well—they're making life into a party. And, they are fighters. Every day they confront an enemy many choose to ignore.

Patti looks over at me, her eyes dancing with amusement and what can only be described as pure delight, she says, "If our mothers could see us now."

68

In New York I don't feel lonely. I eat a hot dog on a bench in the park while my sister is at work. Sometimes I just walk for thirty blocks through expanses of over-crunchy fall leaves and get lost. Once, I wound up along the East River, another time at the Flatiron Building, where I just stopped and gazed up at the odd, skinny shape of the steel-framed structure. *It isn't what it is supposed to be*, I thought. It rose proudly, claiming its place among the other buildings—it couldn't have cared less. With the sun hitting its windows, and a few clouds floating above, I imagine it felt liberated.

This is New York. I've heard this before. But now I understand. No one seems to care who you are or how you do things. It's enough just to be whoever you are. So, in a way, you're never lost, because wherever you are is where you're meant to be, which could be anywhere.

* * *

IT'S A WEDNESDAY NIGHT AND CINDY AND I ARE GOING TO DINNER with her boss, George. But just before leaving, she says that she isn't feeling well. I check her forehead; it's cool. She looks fine. She says she has a bad stomach that came out of nowhere.

"Should we cancel?" I ask.

"No, you go," Cindy says.

I feel bad leaving Cindy home alone but she insists I go.

"You're in New York. You need to have fun."

I think about it. Dinner with George? What will we talk about? I don't know movie advertising, though he did like my opinion about the *Flashdance* poster. But a whole dinner? He is *so* slick and cool and I have nothing in common with him. I decide that I'll just pretend it's an interview for *Newsweek* and keep asking him questions like, "How did you decide to get into film?" and he'll do all the talking. I've been to the White House. If I can dine next to Donald Regan, I can certainly talk to anybody. Anyway, it's generous of George to insist on taking us out—it will be fun, even if it's just me.

Two hours later, the maître d' escorts me to a booth toward the back of the restaurant. As I pass by other diners, hip and elegant couples talking in hushed tones, tables with candles, I once again feel far away from Washington. I am another Pam, the New York Pam, the sexy, non-governmental-relations one. Some might even envy me. Is she in publishing? A writer? Look how she breezes by us, confident and effortlessly cool, like that Charlie perfume ad. If only they knew the effort I'm making. It's as if I'm carrying the other Pam, in her khakis, burdened by sadness and confusion, on my back.

I spot George in a leather jacket, his glasses perched on his nose. As I slip inside the booth, next to him, he kisses me on the cheek. I notice the scent of musk; his skin is smooth. There's a moment of awkwardness as I feel a slight attraction. I quickly push that thought away. This is Cindy's boss. *Just enjoy the evening, like you're on vacation*, I tell myself.

We chat, and a martini soothes my nerves. I don't have to pretend I'm interviewing him for *Newsweek*, because he is asking all the questions.

"Art history major?"

"And French. Double major."

He seems impressed.

I'm surprised at myself for opening up to him so quickly. I tell him about my marriage, how tough it was, Pam's illness, and my father's scandal, which he knows about from Cindy. And he listens, leaning forward on one elbow, looking into my eyes, nodding. It's like he's feeling sorry for me, like he'd like to fix me. He arches one eyebrow as he stares at me, as though he is trying to see who I really am. He touches my arm, another hint of musk wafts upward, and suddenly I get a bolt of headiness from the martini. I have to inhale deeply. I notice his linen shirt, his olive skin, and his dark hair. He is handsome, which I hadn't quite appreciated before. His voice is deep. I breathe in more musk.

This is crazy. I am suddenly nervous. It's just a dinner. He was planning to take me *and* Cindy. She works for him. I am her sister. George appreciates that I am visiting and that I get to be out on the town. And, anyway, I'm reading too much into this. I take in a slow, deep breath to calm myself. I toss out a smile to make sure he's not uncomfortable should he be hit by my bad energy, or if he can somehow read my thoughts. *At all costs, be pleasing*, I tell myself. He's European; they kiss on the cheek. It's not that he is interested in *me*. I've been doing all the talking; I should ask him some questions now. How thoughtless of me. So he's handsome, smells like musk. So what? It's no big deal. Maybe he was looking forward to this, too. He probably needed it.

"I'm so glad *you* don't have a tummy ache," George murmurs.

I am caught off guard. It's the way he says it, slow and suggestive. He is grinning now—nice teeth, white squares. I smell my fragrance mixed with his. A part of me is definitely attracted to him. "A part of me"? No, all of me. The martini doesn't help. Suddenly he puts his hand under my chin and guides my face towards his and he kisses me slowly. His tongue feels cool. I can sense his breath through his nostrils. A piñata just erupted inside of me like the papier-mâché donkey we loved as kids at Christmas on Olvera Street. It explodes in my chest, showering candy and treats into the air and over me. I am dazzled. I don't have a husband anymore. I get to do this. It's not like I'm cheating. *Oh, my God*. Thrilling. *No, I can't*. Yes, I can.

I don't recognize myself, and I don't even need to be looking in a mirror to see this: New York Pam. I am different. I am *being* different. Not the good girl. But *this* is not me. It's irresponsible. George is married with a wife and kids in New Jersey. Did I forget that? But Cindy told me they hardly speak, except when he sees his kids. Maybe they will get back together, and I could be preventing that. I'm awful. Okay, maybe that's okay. It's not my responsibility. My stomach tightens in its familiar way.

In between bites of sole meunière and petits pois à la français, George and I make out. We drink expensive French wine. Everything is in slow motion. I am relaxed again. The taste of butter, his lips. His low, throaty laugh. I am falling.

"Chocolate soufflés," George says to our waiter, pouring more wine. More. I want more. More chocolate, more wine, more him.

George is smooth, and sophisticated. Patrick would not approve; he is so conservative and uptight. Being out and getting drunk with a suave, married man is worse than a moth hole in my sweater. It is not nice.

Robin was the opposite of both George and Patrick, almost like a teenager. He loved gulping down burgers before he ran off for a game of football, leaving me to do the dishes like a dutiful wife. Once, I leaned over the counter to grab something on a high shelf. I hit a knob on the counter drawer. It felt good. I stayed there, slowly moving back and forth, my clitoris poised over the protruding knob. I had an orgasm in our kitchen. My first. Robin barely touched me. He did when we dated, sort of. *Stop thinking about this*, I try to quiet my mind. George is feeding me a bite of soufflé. Why didn't I tell Robin about my kitchen experience? Maybe he would have touched me if I told him I liked it.

After dinner we're in George's limousine. I am standing on the seat through the sunroof, my arms waving to the New York skyline.

"I love New York," I say in slurred tones.

"Eddie, the apartment," George says to his driver.

Same view, high above. City lights and the jeweled evening are surging me forward. We're in bed, and my silk shirt is on the floor.

"God, you're beautiful," he murmurs.

He is a man. I've never been with one—just boys. He smells musky, still. He's warm, not in a hurry. I feel the stubble of his beard between my legs. In his Greek, gravelly voice, he whispers, "I bet your husband never went down on you." *No, he didn't*, I think to myself. He never did that.

My body responds. Another piñata. I am showered with candy and sensual pleasure. I am escaping my old life.

"Marriage takes work," my mother would say when I'd call complaining. So, I would go back to house chores. More dishes, more burgers—but it didn't work. I shoved three quarters of myself away. Now, I'm all me. And it is such fun, I can't believe it.

All these years I wasn't sure I was beautiful. I mean, I could *do* beautiful—wear the right clothes and wash my hair with Herbal Essences shampoo, and let it fall over one eye like when I met Steve McQueen on the beach in California with the Reagans. But I never *felt* beautiful, and I figured once I married I would *be* beautiful because I'd have a husband. But that wasn't the case. And it always confused me, as though I really did have a deficit. But in this moment, I know that's not true. George can't take his eyes off of me. And I am grateful to him more than he probably knows.

69

The next morning, I arrive at my brother Doug's. He has just returned from out of town and opens the door in his terry bathrobe. I smell coffee as he ushers me inside, insisting I have a cup. If only he knew how much I've already had sitting in bed with George, gazing out at the fog and skyscrapers.

"Why are you up so early, seven a.m., dressed?" Doug says, curiously.

"In my clothes from last night, you mean?" I say, smiling. "I'm just coming back."

He looks at me. Then it dawns on him; his eyes widen. I'm toying with my brother and it's fun.

"George," I say slowly, evenly.

"What?" Doug stares at me without blinking.

"It was amazing."

His eyes dart off; I know he's processing what I said.

"It's not such a big deal. Don't be a prude."

"Have you told Cindy?"

"Nope, you were my first stop." I say this as if I were giving him a gift.

There's no reason this should shock him. Doug and Cindy have been doing these things always. Doug had a fling with the wife of a big-deal musician, right after college. He was renting a guesthouse in the Hollywood Hills, writing scripts, not going to law school, all against our father's wishes. They'd smoke pot under the stars at night. Cindy had a director boyfriend who rode a Harley and was in love with his estranged sister. Then she took skydiving lessons and parachuted out of an airplane, spraining her ankle. She was always late for my parents' dinner parties.

Why am I so different? Why did I become so cautious? What was it about me? We're in the same family. We sat at the same dinner table, ate the same tuna casserole my mother made every Sunday. We all listened as our parents warned us not to get into show business: "The people are not good." They didn't listen, but of course, I did.

It's as if I buried my spontaneous and young self. They never had a chance to exist. And why is that? Doing what was safe *was* safe. Safe was being good—my hair combed perfectly, my clothes neat, saying what I thought people wanted to hear. Unsafe was being messy, voicing my opinion, or even *having* an opinion. My siblings were terrified of safe. Or, rather, they weren't terrified of anything.

And I wonder: being terrified, how did it happen? At what point did I veer off course, from the messiness and unpredictability of evolving? Was it when I was little? Was it a moment, or was it several moments? And now, all of a sudden, I am angry. Angry at myself for letting that happen. I've deprived myself of so many opportunities. I'm twenty-eight years old and I don't know who I am meant to be.

70

I can't stop asking myself the question, *Why am I so different than my siblings?* And I don't know the answer, really. But my mother must know. My hand reaches for the phone and I dial her in Washington. Her voice instantly comforts me.

"Mom, I just don't understand, what happened?"

She tells me, in the most loving way, not to be neurotic. She has said this to me my whole life.

"Honey, you are just this way. Ever since you were little. Your father and I worried, but we just smiled, you know, like everything was good."

When did this start? How did I get this way? I search my mind as I hang up the phone. When I was little? I don't remember *not* being this way.

The thing I most remember after the dining chair incident in our house is math class in high school. I was trying to understand a geometry problem on the blackboard, when all of a sudden, I was hit by a blast of fear. Terrified, I had asked to be excused, to run to the bathroom. But my teacher Mrs. Rubenstein demanded I stay in my seat. I did for a minute because I was scared of her. Then I jumped up and ran out to the hallway to escape, never making it to the bathroom. Instead, I'd passed out on the linoleum floor in front of the hallway lockers.

This happened so many times in Berkeley as well. I was older, it was worse; it happened more often. In my art history lecture in Evans Hall, I always sat next to the door in case I had a panic attack. One time the professor surprised us with a quiz. I felt unprepared. I felt caught off guard. What if I didn't know all the answers? What if I failed? I panicked. I had to leave. Students stared at me as I grabbed my books and ran out the door. They could tell something was wrong, and I was embarrassed.

Then another time, in French class, I stopped writing in my blue book, in which we took exams, and asked to be excused because I couldn't come up with the right answers and I didn't want my teacher to give me a bad grade. And I also didn't want to disappoint my father. I had to retake my final exam.

I notice a drop of turquoise paint on the floor from when my sister painted one wall in her kitchen. Did it concern her that the turquoise color might be too bold on her wall? No, she is not concerned—and, for that matter, she's not even fearful of most things. But doesn't everyone have some kind of fear at some time or another? Do they just move around it or through it? I ask Cindy about this, and she says at times she is afraid of things but is able to step over her fear. Sometimes, however, she admits, it's just not possible.

I want to say these four words to myself—"just don't be afraid"— so that I can climb out from where I've been, to open my arms wide, and float, weightless, unencumbered by limitation, to be big instead of small, to make my own mark in the world and to know it is genuinely mine, not a copied version handed to me.

My parents have no fear. Well, sometimes they do, but they don't allow it to consume them. They stand up to fear. They make their mark in the world.

Don't be afraid, I repeat silently to myself. It's my turn.

71

The real problem with fear is that it keeps me small. It prevents me from choosing what *I* want. Instead, fear makes me ask, What does *my mother* want? What do *my parents* want? What does *society* want? Conforming, fitting in—that's safe. I carry my mother's Judith Leiber jewel-encrusted purse like a shield. I marry the congressman's son. I follow the well-lit path my parents created. Fear moves me to safety like a cattle dog. I try to venture out, cross over to new terrain, but fear nips at my heels. It herds me back into the known. Fear makes me take the social temperature in the room and adjust myself accordingly. I'm a reflection of whatever surrounds me. I squeeze myself into someone else's template. I'm good at this.

This year, though, has shown me that fear didn't do its job: It didn't keep me safe. Even though I did all the right things, I still wasn't safe. My perfect marriage ended in divorce, and my mentor and best friend became terminally ill.

As I think about fear and safety and rules and expectations—or rather, as I think about how to find the courage I need to reinvent my life—my father comes to my mind. If anyone should have been fearful this year, it's him. The world hates him. Still, he gets up every day for breakfast, puts on a tie, and goes to the office. He pushes past the reporters, holds his head high, and forges ahead. People talk about him behind his back and in the papers. He could just stay at home. But he doesn't. My father is brave, I realize, because he has to be. He's ambitious. He demands a lot from himself, which requires him to put up with fear. The things he wants to do are accompanied by fear. And so he overcomes it, or pushes it aside, to do what he needs to do.

Of all things, I'm reminded of Dad's acquaintance with Winston Churchill. He knew the former British prime minister early in his career, when he was a talent agent and television producer and lived with my mother in New York. He hired Churchill's daughter Sarah, an actress, to appear in a television series he was producing in England. Then he arranged for her to cover her father's election for CBS radio, when Churchill ran a second time for prime minister. For Dad, the highlight of the whole experience was when he was invited into Churchill's home. They met in his bedroom, where Churchill sat on his bed, papers surrounding him. He always worked on his bed. It was so intimate. He said when Churchill looked at him, it was like the prime minister stopped blinking. My father loved Churchill's devotion as a father, his razor-sharp wit, his utter fearlessness. He loved to quote the former prime minister: "Fear is a reaction. Courage is a decision."

* * *

I SPEND THE NEXT DAY THINKING ABOUT MAKING THE DECISION to be brave. It feels empowering. At H&H Bagels, a man steps in front of me in line. I politely tell him, "You'll have to wait your turn." In the pouring rain, I ask a woman to move her wet purse from a deli counter stool so I can sit. I speak up for myself, practicing being in the world in a brave, albeit small, way. Yet, I don't feel a shift. I still feel uneasy.

At a coffee shop near my sister's apartment the next morning, I see a young woman eating alone, reading a paperback. She looks comfortable in her own skin—glasses, messy ponytail, unafraid of what people think of her. I had tried that once in Washington—I had gone out for pancakes by myself and sat alone at a table. I'd never even opened my book because I was too worried people were staring at me and judging me for sitting without company.

I was always worried about what other people said and thought of me. I feel like ever since my father's stapler went missing, I've made the underneath of the calming floral dining chair my hiding spot. I've hidden from authority figures. My father was the first authoritative figure in my life, and yet, since him, I feel like I've somehow been drawn to authoritative personalities. My parents had primed me to be the perfect wife that I thought I became when I married Robin. I had unconsciously decided he was "the man of the house." He practically replaced my father, and I was the one who had put him in charge. Then it was Patrick, who made me feel like it was blasphemy to have a moth hole in my sweater and who decided on my behalf that I would never work after marrying him. But this was my idea of feeling safe—being in the shadow of those who commanded authority. I handed them that power over me.

I came to believe that my identity depended on male figures, as if I wasn't enough. I have associated authoritative figures with men, but now when I think about it, I realize that most of the women in my life were also equally imposing if not more so—starting with my mother. Then, in school, it was my math teacher Mrs. Rubenstein, and then Nancy Reynolds and Anne Wexler at work. And even if Pam and Cindy didn't control me, I felt like they had taken me under their wing and taught me how to do life. They had made me feel safe and protected.

My mother made it sound that way when I called her: "Your father and I worried about you." Fear has informed my choices, time and time again.

I want to be like Pam, who faces a life-threatening illness with such courage. She even took the time to put on pearls in the hospital. I would have given up; why do *anything*? I can't imagine how frightening it is for her. Yet she has never lost her sense of humor. I still remember

Pam's good advice. Fill my Filofax with appointments, fight for a cause I believe in, and buy a new scarf. I want to do this so badly, and yet I feel frozen, kind of immobilized.

When I was nineteen and leaving for college, my father was driving me to the airport in his powder-blue Lincoln Continental on a drizzly Los Angeles morning. My suitcases were piled in the trunk. I was thinking about my new school year, new classes, a new roommate, trying to figure out my major, and I was overcome with fear. Art history? What if I really want classes but they're not available? What if my new roommate and I don't get along?

Dad could tell that rather than being excited, I was scared.

"It's okay to be scared."

His brows were drawn together as he glanced over at me. The windshield wipers *swish-swashing* back and forth, the rain coming down harder; Dad looking back at the road—moments went by.

How is this helping me? I thought. I knew he was trying to make me feel better, but it wasn't working.

"Listen to me," he said. "Have you ever felt this way before?"

He asked me to really answer the question and so I thought about it. Of course, I had felt this way before. Hundreds of times.

"And you got through it."

Well, I had, actually. Every time, I realized.

"And you'll feel this way again," he said. "And you'll get through it, again. Feeling this way is temporary," he told me.

He said that my fear is like passing weather, ever changing. But for me, it has always been a dark cloud with no silver lining.

* * *

WHAT'S IT LIKE TO BE FEARLESS? To not care about what people are saying about you? Or if you do care, to not let it consume you. To not care about eating alone in a restaurant, to not care that you are divorced.

I ask myself these questions on my last day in New York. My sister and I have just left a Warhol exhibition in the Village. Normally we'd take a cab back to her apartment, but it's rush hour and the streets are gridlocked. So my sister asks me the question I have been dreading hearing the entire time I've been in New York.

"Want to get the subway?"

I hesitate. Just the thought of climbing down those stairs into the dark makes me want to hyperventilate. I'm afraid I'll have a panic attack, and I won't know how to escape back through the turnstile and up the stairs fast enough.

I remember my father's words. I've felt this way before, and I will again. I hear the windshield wipers swish back and forth in his Lincoln Continental. It is just passing bad weather. I beg the clouds of my anxiety to pass. I know they will, but I have to help.

I turn to my sister, and almost in a slow-motion moment of my own personal triumph, I say, "Yes." A final wave of anxiety and near-panic washes over me, and, to my delight, I'm still standing. Small steps.

And maybe it's as simple as that. I need to start saying yes to things that scare me. That's it. I will not magically become a different Pam. But I have to begin somewhere.

72

Shortly after I return to Washington, Ronald Reagan is reelected, winning by a landslide. His inauguration takes place inside the Capitol Rotunda, an imposing, domed, circular space, over a hundred feet high, a painted fresco of George Washington ascending to the heavens visible through the oculus of the dome. I stand with my family, just a few rows behind the president and Mrs. Reagan. My father is beaming; my mother, elegant and visibly moved. I try to remind myself of the historical moment I am living through. This date will be an important milestone in American history.

Cabinet members, senators, and congressmen stand, influential-looking, posing for photographs. And then I notice something that the cameras won't catch. Mrs. R shifts her adoring gaze from her husband to glance in our direction. I see her eyes meet my mother's, and I recognize a knowing exchange between two best friends. There is so much meaning between them in this brief moment. I almost feel as if I am intruding by observing it.

They started in California, in the carpool line. Now, they are at the center of world power.

As I watch them, I feel such affection for both women. They have earned this moment.

But it is their moment. I realize that this is *their* party, not mine. This whole time, I have just been along for the ride.

And then this moment becomes my own. I make the decision to act on my own behalf; I decide to move back to California. I want to go home. I am ready to start over, whatever that might mean for me.

Ten Years Later

California allowed me to begin again. I rented an apartment in a 1940s stucco walkup, in the unglamorous part of Beverly Hills. I found a job at a small PR firm. If I craned my neck, I could see the Hollywood Sign atop the Santa Monica mountains. I wrote press releases for clients, the USC business school, Swarovski Crystal (then a small company), and a clothing brand. The work was routine. No one pointed out (only occasionally) that I was Charlie Wick's daughter. No one asked if I knew the president. At night, I perched on the tiny stair landing off my kitchen overlooking the alley, the air scented with night-blooming jasmine. I thought about my life. It's not so much that I replayed the past, but rather it replayed itself. It unwound itself, it unspooled, the experiences releasing themselves from the tension of being so tightly wound. They began to reoccupy a space inside of me where they no longer gripped me so fiercely. It was a letting go. As my past loosened its grip, I discovered the me that had been underneath the tightness. As if I had been sealed inside, as if moving back to California was some prehistoric archaeological dig. I was unearthed.

I found many things. I found myself taking a stand-up comedy class taught by a comedian in a Venice bungalow. It didn't seem out of the ordinary. Everyone I worked with did something other than a day job.

One coworker, a would-be actor, kept 8x10 glossy head shots in his briefcase just in case; another woman took operatic voice lessons at night. The idea of trying stand-up just didn't feel unnatural to me. And while some fear was present, this was a fear I chose.

* * *

TONIGHT, THE LINE IS AROUND THE BLOCK. The Improv in Hollywood is a legendary comedy club. My comedy class is performing. A night for novices. We have written our routines. We have rehearsed. We are prepared. In our class, where we learned stand-up is personal, we wrote our own material. I have memorized my set, I know my jokes. About LA. About Washington. About married life and divorce.

Later, I watch as several of my classmates perform their routines. I can tell they are nervous. One neatly groomed guy, awkward and anxious, a pharmacist by day, forgets his opening punchline. An otherwise confident (to the point of being annoying) bespectacled paralegal in our class looks like she is going to cry. Finally, it's my turn.

"*Pam Wick!*" The bald and tattooed MC announces me. I freeze for a second. My heart leaps. I am excited, nervous. I walk toward the stage. Deep breath. Whistles and applause. An enthusiastic audience, friends and family and strangers. People drinking, eating, the smell of pizza and booze.

I am momentarily back in Washington. At the White House. Walking up the steps with my parents. My dad takes my hand as he ushers me and my mother to the entrance. He turns to me, beaming. "Darling, it's showtime!"

The applause brings me back. I continue up the stairs to the stage, stairs I never imagined climbing. A wave of dread washes over me. I wait for it to pass. I step onto the stage and into my own life.

THE END

Acknowledgments

I am enormously grateful to my husband Richard, for your enthusiasm, counsel, and patience. You listened and considered every word of my memoir, never tiring of your assignment. I love you.

To my sister Cynthia, you are my truth serum. Your objectivity and honesty raised the level of my craft. We joke that we share the same heartbeat. Thanks for all the love on this ride.

Such gratitude to my brother Doug, for always championing me. From your film set on Malta, when you called me to tell me you couldn't put down my manuscript, to recruiting Lucy and Tessa to help me with great notes, I am forever heartened.

Sharing a childhood bedroom with my sister Kim, cemented our friendship for life. Thank you, my dear sister, for brightening the tough days and for always being there.

To Chan, thank you for a lifetime of advice and love.

To Wendy Dale, my writing coach. I remain in awe of your ability to find the gold inside of me. Not only are you a published author of your own memoir, but you are the most tenacious, smart, kind person I know.

I owe endless thanks to my literary agent Michael Carlisle, who championed my book from day one.

To Gretchen Young my publisher and Madeline Sturgeon my editor, your guidance and vision, as well as your patience, are invaluable.

The Reagan family, you will always be a cozy Christmas Eve to me. Our forty-year family history is a through line in my life.

My many supportive friends (you know who you are) who never stopped asking about my book, who never seemed exasperated by 'it's not done yet.' You have blessed me tenfold. I am grateful for each and every one of you who have played a role in bringing my memoir to life.